Kingfisher

Tales from the Halcyon River

EVANS
MITCHELL
BOOKS

Kingfisher

Tales from the Halcyon River

Written and photographed by **Charlie Hamilton James**

For Philippa
– the other bird in my life!

Publishers
Evans Mitchell Books
The Old Forge
16 Church Street
Rickmansworth, Herts
WD3 1DH United Kingdom
info@embooks.co.uk
www.embooks.co.uk

© Evans Mitchell Books 2009

Text & Photographs
© Charlie Hamilton James 2009

Editor Caroline Taggart

Design Darren Westlake at **TU ink**
www.tuink.co.uk

Origination, Printing and Binding
Passavia, Germany

ISBN 978-1-901268-38-6

Contents

Foreword by
Simon King

The British Isles are not world renowned for their exotic avifauna. The term Ellbeejay (LBJ, or Little Brown Job), used to describe the vast majority of birds in Britain, is not an English one by coincidence.

There are, of course, a few exceptions to the ranks of beige and dun-coloured birds that flit across these shores; goldfinch, yellowhammer, jay and a few waterfowl all add a splash of colour to an otherwise monochrome pallet of feathers. But none comes anywhere close to the subject of this book.

The kingfisher is a world-ranking dandy of a bird. It is not simply the intensity of its colour, but the startling mix of blue, white, black and orange-red that makes this little spirit of rivers, lakes and streams one of the most kaleidoscopic on the planet. Yet despite being anything but cryptic, it is rarely seen. This is in part due to its habits, flying fast and low along a watercourse so that only a chance glance in the right direction is likely to reveal it; in part due to a character which shuns the gaze and company of man. Even once you become familiar with its shrill, piping call, a sound that heralds its arrival around a bend in a river, the best view you are likely to get is that of a startling bolt of cobalt blue as it flashes past you and disappears from sight.

All the more extraordinary, then, that the following pages reveal not simply portraits of this living jewel, but an intimate account of its life history. Making a fine photographic image of a kingfisher is challenging enough; capturing moments of intimacy, from aggression to courtship, hunting to raising a family, takes a very special kind of person. And Charlie Hamilton James is one such soul.

Charlie first contacted me when he was a boy, telling me about the kingfishers he watched on a stream near his home on the edge of Bristol in the south of England. Some years later, I had the honour of presenting him with the Young Wildlife Photographer of the Year award and subsequently have watched him develop into one of the world's leading wildlife film-makers and photographers. He and I have worked together closely on many projects and I am lucky now to be able to call him my friend. We have shared many

an evening when his wit and laconic sense of humour have had me in tears of laughter but, for all his air of casual indifference, Charlie possesses a quality that sets him apart from most mortals. For when most of us have thrown in the towel due to bad weather, bad luck or just sheer exhaustion, he goes on, determined to see the unseen, to reveal the unexpected, to witness the unique.

It is thanks to this mix of knowledge, passion, dogged perseverance and a healthy splash of obsession that we can now share the astonishing images that grace the pages of this book. For most of us, the scenes here will remain an enigma, a hidden and tantalising promise of the magic that shines just out of reach, beyond the next bend in the stream. But we will know it could be there, and all be the richer for it.

Opposite: **The Manor male fishing the Court field**

So when the Shadows laid asleep
From underneath these Banks do creep,
And on the River as it flows
With Eben Shuts begin to close:
The modest Halcyon comes in sight,
Flying betwixt the Day and Night:
And such an horror calm and dumb,
Admiring Nature does benum.

Andrew Marvell, Upon Appleton House, to my Lord Fairfax

A life with kingfishers

When I was six I drew a picture of a kingfisher for my teacher at school. I didn't know it was called a kingfisher until my sister told me, but from that moment on I have been completely obsessed. When I was 14 I began skipping school to watch kingfishers; by the time I was 15 I barely ever went to school. Instead I would wave my mum goodbye and trot off to the bus station in central Bristol in my school uniform. I would change on the bus and jump off it sometime later to vanish into the woods by the river.

There I would spend my days huddled under an old Land-rover tarpaulin munching on sandwiches and watching kingfishers. I got to know the river intimately, every rivulet, every pool. I knew where the trout hid, how to catch bullheads with my hands, where the fox slept in the sun, where the weasels lived and, most importantly, where my beloved kingfishers hung out. Just before three in the afternoon I would hop back onto the bus and get home in time not to arouse suspicion. My mother was no fool, though. As I trotted through the door at the end of my long day she would ask, 'So where did you go today?' and I would tell her. Academically I was a disaster, but by the time I left school I knew an awful lot about small blue birds.

Today I am still obsessed with kingfishers and, despite having spent thousands of hours watching them from my hide, I still get a buzz of excitement every time I see one.

It is therefore no coincidence that I now live in an old mill-worker's cottage by the river I spent my youth on. Every day I watch the kingfishers zipping up and down the river from my kitchen window and in the mornings I lie in bed and listen to them whistling excitedly to each other. So my house is now my hide and it gives me an incredible glimpse into the life of these spectacular little birds.

This book is two things. It is a personal monograph on kingfishers and it is a photographic study. In my early teens I was very keen to take my obsession with kingfishers beyond just observation, so I started attempting to photograph them. In those early days I was astoundingly unsuccessful at getting any photographs of any worth, but I developed an interest in photography which I have pursued into a career. This book is the culmination of all the work and time I have put into watching kingfishers over the last 20 years. However, almost all the photographs you see have been taken since 2004. My intention when photographing kingfishers has always been to show them as they look to me, set in the context of their environment. Kingfishers are tiny blue jewels along the river. That is how I want to show them to you.

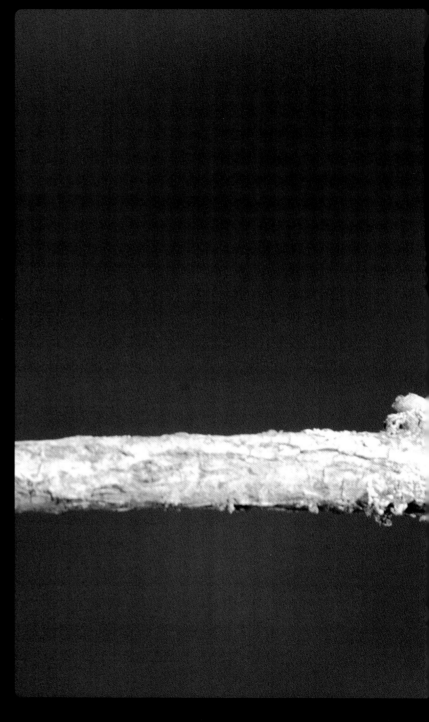

THE HALCYON RIVER

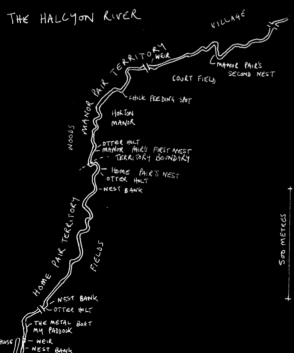

This book also serves to deliver a passion of mine onto a page. The little brook in the West Country where I work with the kingfishers has always been a huge inspiration to me. It is nothing special, just another slither of water slipping through fields and villages, bubbling under roads, past pubs and factories and draining sewage works. But on a bright dawn in spring, there is nowhere else on earth I would rather be, squatting in my hide and sipping my coffee, listening to the trickle of the water as it tumbles over itself and the piping of the wagtails as they busy about. I love the sound of the trickle, I love the earthy smell of the river when it floods and I love never knowing what secrets it will reveal to me next. It is a perfect little marker of the seasons and the perfect backdrop for watching kingfishers. In this book I shall call it the Halcyon River, but I shall not reveal its true name and I beg you not to try to discover it. It is no more special than any other river in Britain.

Perhaps what has just happened while I have been sitting at my screen trying to explain myself to you says it all. It is nine in the evening, dusk, and my concentration has just been stolen from the computer by a faint whistling outside. It sounded like an otter. I ran downstairs from my office to the kitchen and looked out the window, just in time to see an otter pop up under the bridge that leads to my front door. I sneaked outside with my wife and we peered over the railings by the river to watch a young otter munching a fish. It chewed for a moment, then rolled under the water and swam right beneath us. It popped up again a few metres downriver, turned to look at us and vanished.

Left: A fish-eye view – perhaps the last thing the fish ever sees! Above: A protective blue membrane passes over the kingfisher's eye as it hits the water.

Moments like that, when the river reveals another secret to us, are special and cherished. And it is the not knowing what will be unfolded next that makes time spent here so rewarding.

I don't know what first attracted me to kingfishers; perhaps it was their colour. That incredible pallet of turquoise, blue and orange sets the kingfisher apart from all other British birds, making it appear tropical. Indeed, our little kingfisher is as much a bird of the tropics as it is of the northern hemisphere. *Alcedo atthis* – the Common Kingfisher – has a geographic range extending across Europe to North Africa, east through Russia and China to Japan, then south to the islands of Indonesia and beyond, making it the most widespread of all the kingfishers. Most of this book is concerned with *Alcedo atthis ispida*, the northern European subspecies of the Common Kingfisher, as it is this bird that we see on rivers and streams in Britain.

Far left: **The House male on the edge of the Manor territory.** Above: **The Manor female watches for fish in the wood.** Above right: **The Manor male.**

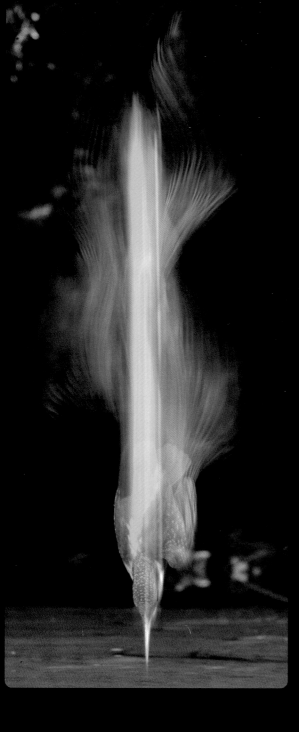

There are 86 full species of kingfisher worldwide. They are spread in a band around the tropics, with the majority occurring in Africa, Asia and Australia. South America has five species, North America only one. They vary from the drab to the spectacular; some, such as the Shovel Billed Kingfisher, barely look like kingfishers at all and others are so exotic they could be mistaken for birds of paradise. They range in size from the tiniest Dwarf and Pygmy Kingfishers to the comparatively enormous Giant Kingfishers and kookaburras. In my travels around the globe I have attempted to photograph some of these more exotic species and I have devoted a couple of chapters to them later in the book.

This book spans roughly a year and it tells the story of two pairs of kingfishers – the House pair, whose territory includes the river outside my house, and the Manor pair, whose territory includes the Manor garden 1500 m (1 mile) or so upriver. The story starts in winter.

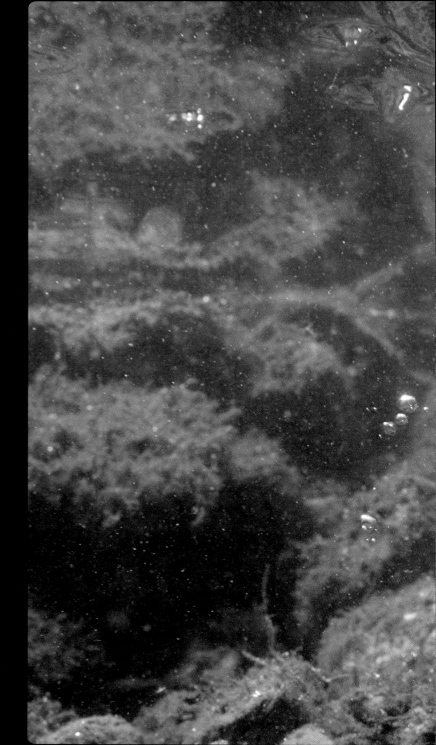

Far left: A kingfisher dive is incredibly fast.
This picture shows the distance travelled
in one eighth of a second.
Left: Air clings to the kingfisher underwater,
helping it to keep dry and aiding buoyancy.
Above: Within a second of leaving the perch
the kingfisher will be back with a fish.

Above: **The Manor female hunting in the Court field at dawn.**

Listening for the **whistle**

I watched the female kingfisher speed bullet-like over the weir and up the Court field stretch. She shone like a blue jewel against the brown murk of the swollen river and the drab dead reeds that sulked in clumps along its edge. She whistled as she rounded the corner at the end of the stretch. A moment later another kingfisher sped over the weir, headed up the Court field stretch and alighted in the dark bow of an ash tree. It whistled once. It wasn't an aggressive whistle, but at this time of year it should have been.

6 January

I am intrigued. There are two kingfishers sharing a fishing spot in the Court field, in the upper edge of the Manor territory. It seems too early in the year for a pair of kingfishers to be tolerating each other so closely, so what's happening? At the top end of the Manor territory the river slips under a road bridge. Above the bridge is a long strip of deep water flowing through what I call the court field. It is perfect for kingfishers and there is a lay-by next to the bridge where I can park. I spend a while watching the birds through my binoculars from the car. They sit quite happily next to each other, even on the same branch, fishing and preening. Kingfishers are highly territorial, especially on small rivers like this, and should not, by my understanding, be behaving in this way. I decide to set up a hide and find out what's going on.

Early morning – my favourite time – the river is bathed in crisp moonlight...

7 January

6 am It is still dark and I am trudging across the pony field above the manor to my hide. The dark shapes of the horses watch me from the gloom. It is freezing cold; a thick covering of frost that could be mistaken for a light covering of snow lies over the land. I wonder why I got up so early that it is still too dark to see anything. 'I like to be ready for the light,' I convince myself, although the only light around now is coming from the moon! I set my hide up beneath the ash tree in whose low boughs the mysterious pair of kingfishers has been sitting; I ready my camera and flash guns and settle in.

It is not long before a kingfisher lands quietly in the ash tree and scouts for fish. The light is forgiving enough now to allow me to identify the bird as an adult female. I don't know her, as this territory is not the one that passes my house. She is relaxed with the hide, though, and for a while she sits quietly in the gloom. She catches two very small fish and eats them.

Left: Kingfisher feathers have no blue pigment. The colour comes from oils reflecting light.

Above: The Manor female was able to tolerate another female overwintering in her territory.

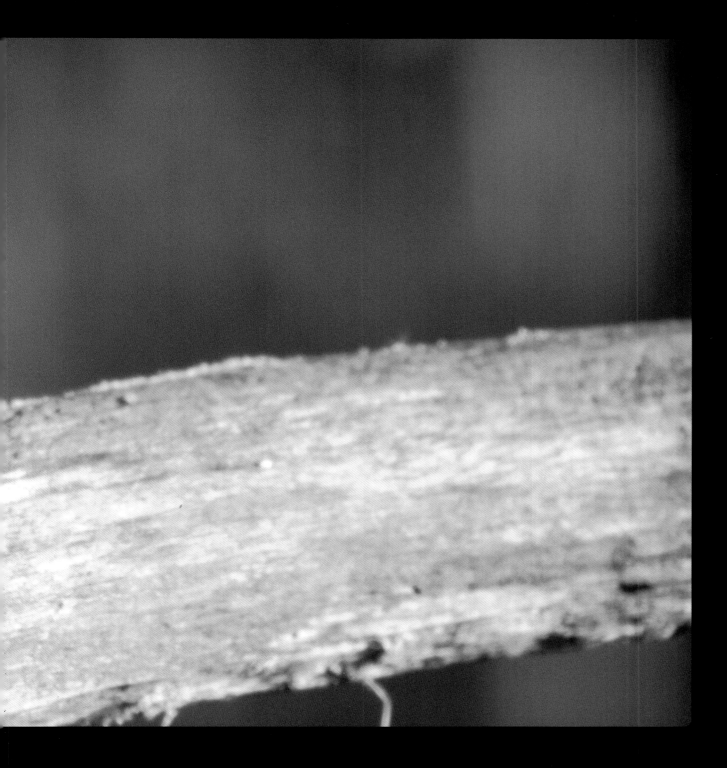

An hour later she's still sitting there. I wonder where the other bird is. Perhaps fishing somewhere upriver. This is a very quiet time of year for kingfishers; they have little to think about but themselves and so there is little to disturb them but the odd territorial dispute or flood.

A faint whistling upriver suggests another bird. I wait, poised for it to appear, but it doesn't. I expect the female I am watching to become agitated and adopt an aggressive posture, but she doesn't. Instead she flies over to a branch closer to my hide and searches for fish. I take a couple of shots of her in the increasing light. She is very obviously an adult female. Her lower mandible is almost entirely orange.

Above right: I assume it was the young female's first winter.

A while later the whistling comes again, and a moment after that the other bird. It lands in the ash bough and whistles its arrival. The female whistles back, but neither bird seems aggressive. This is very odd behaviour. I look at the other bird's bill and see no orange on the lower mandible, so I identify it as a male. This makes perfect sense: kingfishers will often pair for several years, sharing a territory with each other during the breeding season and parts of it at other times – though rarely without an amount of animosity when they're not breeding. The male bird flies over and lands next to the female. She whistles in slight alarm and moves down the perch a little. On closer inspection the male seems to have a slither of orange on his lower beak. It's not as bold as the female's but it is definitely there. Which can only mean that this bird is also a female.

Left: The young female with a minnow. **Above:** An adult female showing her red lower mandible. Males and juveniles have black bills.

27

I watch it through the lens for a while and take a few snaps. The original female catches a fish and flies off, whistling as she lands in a nearby tree. I can only assume that what I'm looking at is a first-year female, whose beak is not yet fully orange, and that the two birds are overwintering together. I have never heard of kingfishers of the same sex overwintering together in Britain, certainly not on such a small river. It is possible that the birds are related, mother and daughter perhaps, although I wouldn't attribute their being together to relatedness: kingfisher parents chase their young from their territory at an early age, and the gap between fledging and this winter pairing would be too long for a mother to endure her daughter. If they are related they probably aren't aware of it.

I watch the birds for a few more weeks on and off. By the middle of February the younger bird is gone.

Left: Reflection from the oils in the feathers produces this stunning blue. Above: The House female was quite capable of catching her own fish!   29

26 February

Dawn. I always start work at dawn, preferably before dawn, depending on how often the kids woke me in the night, how late I stayed up and how much I drank. An hour before sunrise is best, though today there is no sun, just a few pink clouds amongst a bruised mass of grey. My hide is very low and I am shooting pictures through a hole just 60 cm (2 ft) off the ground, which forces me to sit on the earth and get repetitively spiked in the arse by brambles. Fortunately I am in my garden, so I have hot coffee on tap! The male bird sits on his perch and watches the minnows below. It is cold, not much above freezing, and the fish lurk amongst the twigs and silt of the riverbed, just out of reach. The bird is patient, though, and relaxed. I am not. It is very difficult to relax in a hide and it is usually very uncomfortable. My aim this morning is to photograph the male bird courtship-feeding the female. This is something I have filmed several times before, but never managed to photograph. I have a couple of flash guns set up, aimed at where the action should happen. Now I have to sit and hope.

Left and above: The House pair courting: courtship-feeding is critical to pair-bonding.

I have been watching this same male for several weeks now, since the middle of January. He has a mate (although he has not consummated the relationship yet) and from the kitchen window I can see them chasing each other in high-speed pursuit up and down the river, whistling with repetitive single peeps. Sometimes they fly high over the house and trees below the weir, then swoop down to the river beyond the mill. Several times I have watched the male fly up out of the water below the weir, across the garden behind my office, over the roof, over the river, out over the paddock, down the road, then back over my garage and lawn before swooping down and alighting next to the female, who watches from a small perch below the weir. He always arrives back to a hail of

whistling from his admirer, then speeds off and does it again. I guess it serves to display his physical prowess.

This morning is quiet, though, and the kingfisher is still. He watches the fishes and thins his body into a dart shape as they flicker beneath him, drawing his feathers in and readying his body for a dive. He can't help doing this, whether he is going to dive or not; like a cat he responds to certain stimuli, the flicker of a fish's tail being the most powerful. He relaxes and preens a little, then stops for a while and watches the blackbirds in the conifer trees above the river heckling the two tawny owls that live beneath the dense dark boughs. The kingfisher never seems to be bothered by the owls; perhaps he knows they are only a real threat to him when he is sleeping.

Above: The House female reflected in the river as she fishes at dawn.

Above: Close inspection reveals a glorious palette of colours!

A faint whistle downriver causes him to spring to attention. His feathers pull in tight, his tail fans slightly and he leans his head out, whistling. The whistles bounce backwards and forwards for a few seconds before the female arrives and settles on the perch next to him. The male retains his aggressive posture and turns his head snake-like to the female, whistling at her. The whistles switch from being single peeps to a double whistle, high then low in pitch and repetitive.

The female responds with similar calls and immediately looks into the river for fish. The male drops his guard a moment later and he too looks for a fish. The female locks onto one. She leans forward poised, holds the pose for a few seconds, then in a flash dives. A split second later she returns with nothing. She shakes herself, spins on her perch and scans the water again.

The male too locks on to a fish. He is more spontaneous than the female: within a second of spotting a potential meal he dives. The female erupts into whistles as the male lands back up on the perch, clutching a fish. She turns to him and whistles single high-pitched peeps as he turns the fish in his beak and batters its head on the branch.

I ready myself now, check my exposures are right and get focus. This is the moment I am waiting for, the 'fish pass'. The moment when the male feeds the female, a confirmation of engagement. My heart races as he finishes dispatching the fish and turns it in his beak so that he may offer it to the female head first. But she is too impatient for him; she has spotted another fish. Before the male has even had time to make his move the female is back on the perch dealing with her own minnow. The male sits with his fish in his bill as the female swallows hers. He watches her patiently, perhaps as disappointed as I am. He chirps to her but she is not interested – perhaps she is full – and she flies off upriver, whistling. The male sits for nearly ten minutes with his fish before turning it round and eating it himself.

Above: The House pair. The arrival of one would always spark an aggressive response from the other.

Above: If the fish moves mid-dive the kingfisher will hover briefly whilst readjusting.

29 February

It is not until my fourth morning in the hide that the male is finally successful. I think perhaps not for the first time, though. The birds are visiting the perch by the hide less frequently. When they do appear, their beaks are muddy. I know what this means: they are digging a nest. February seems very early to me. Normally I would expect them to start digging in early March, but this year it is mild.

The female is first to arrive, followed shortly afterwards by the male. They seem more relaxed with each other, with only a hint of aggression from the female as the male lands on the perch next to her. He catches a fish almost immediately. She watches and peeps to him as he dispatches it on the branch. He turns the fish and her whistling becomes more excited. He watches her for a moment, then shuffles along his perch until he is next to her. He leans towards her, offering the fish; she leans into him and grabs it while he still holds it in his beak. After a brief tussle the birds break free of each other. The female swallows the fish and the male sits bolt upright and fans his tail. This posture seems to serve as both courtship display and aggressive display. Within a few seconds the male is whistling away upriver. The female sits and preens and I check my shots. I've got it! It's out of focus, though. As the birds leant in to each other for the fish pass they moved from side to side and I didn't keep my focus – I have only myself to blame for that.

Above: **The mud on the House male's beak proves that he has been digging a nest.**

This pattern of courtship-feeding continued for several weeks and although I stopped trying to photograph it I could hear the tell-tale whistling of the birds together on the perch while I was out in the garden. Courtship-feeding can last well into the summer, and it appears to me that as it becomes more frequent it is usually instigated by the female. On a few occasions I have even seen the female attempt to feed the male, although only once successfully.

During this time I often followed the birds to find out where they were digging. At first this was in the bank below the weir, just 50 m (50 yds) or so from my kitchen. Then they moved upriver to investigate the artificial nest bank I had made in my paddock. After that they moved to several more potential banks before finally settling on one on the edge of the upper reaches of their territory. It was a location that would, in the coming months, cause them serious problems.

Clockwise from top left: **Courtship-feeding continues throughout the breeding season; the House female with a good-sized minnow; the House female; the House male.**

Dawn in the Manor Garden

The season of hope

Dawn in the wood is like a secret between me and nature. While the world lies in slumber nature lets go a few of her secrets and occasionally rewards the patient with an otter!

6 March

D awn is an hour away and I am slugging through wet grass laden down with camera bags and tripods. My arms are so overloaded that I keep dropping bits of kit. Why I don't do it in two runs I don't know – I am either idle or a fool. Two roe deer watch me, stock still, as I cross the Manor garden and make my way towards the river. They bolt when I make eye contact with them and vanish into the woods. I reach the river. She is dark and gentle at this time of the morning. I lurk behind an elder and silently look towards the nest bank. No-one's at home.

A kingfisher whistles a couple of hundred metres downriver. It's a small, excited burst of whistling – the bird must just have alighted on a perch to fish. I step onto the wet stones and wade out across a small rapid. Something catches my eye halfway across; the dark back of an otter slips under water. I watch a small bow wave as it moves downstream.

The male kingfisher appears suddenly and whistles as he lands on the perch outside the nest. I stand rigid: he can't see me, vegetation blocks his view. The otter pops up just short of the rapid above the nest bank. The kingfisher peers down at the otter and watches her as she shoots the rapid beneath him. As she reaches the pool at the bottom of the rapid, she dives and vanishes. There is a holt just below the pool; perhaps it belongs to her. The kingfisher loses interest and spots me. He flies off, whistling in alarm. I've been caught! I know him well, though, and he knows me. I sneak into my hide, amongst the branches of a small beech tree opposite the nest bank. I set up my tripod, slip my lens through the hide window, arrange the furniture and sit down. I'm barely settled before the kingfisher is back.

Above: The House male fishes with mud still on his beak.

He lands in a pile of sticks forced up against an ash tree during the last flood. He eyes me briefly. I freeze; he's waiting for the slightest movement to confirm his suspicions, but I don't give him one. He settles after a moment and stares upriver to the nest bank. He bobs slightly, thins his feathers tight to his body and hops off his perch. A split second later he alights on his favourite perch just outside the nest he's been digging.

He checks up and down the river, gives me another look over and, when he is satisfied, turns and flies up into the nest chamber. For a couple of minutes the only sound is the bubbling rapid below the nest and the only sign of the kingfisher is the occasional spray of mud from the nest hole. Then a sudden spirited whistling announces the arrival of the female. She looks about excitedly and the male pops out of the nest, whistling to her and hopping

on to the perch next to her. She immediately adopts an aggressive posture, stretching her body to full length and fanning her tail. She drops the pose almost instantly, though, as she recognises him, then turns and flies into the nest hole. The male whistles her in and then goes quiet. He looks over at me, his beak thick with mud. Kingfishers, normally so proud of their perfection, always look comical when they break the spell like this.

Above: After feeding the female, the male fans his tail feathers aggressively. **Right:** Another aggressive posture, a slight dropping of the wings.

A minute later the female is out of the nest and the male is back in so fast that without the excited whistling I would barely have noticed the changeover. She sits quietly as he digs for another few minutes. This pattern of taking turns to dig continues for nearly an hour. The male does the lion's share of the work, perhaps to compensate for all the incubating his partner is about to endure. Suddenly the birds vanish, the female first and then the male, off to feed themselves and check the territory for intruders.

The male returns 20 minutes later and almost immediately starts digging again. In and out, every five minutes. Eventually he tires and sits quietly on the perch outside the nest. A ripple catches my eye out of the side window of my hide. I scan the water. I look out the front window – the otter! She spins about the pool below the rapid, then slips up it. Halfway up she stops and sniffs up the bank. The kingfisher sits 1 m (3 ft) above her head and watches her. She satisfies her nose, continues up the rapid and – in the words of Henry Williamson from *Tarka the Otter* – she vanishes 'smooth as oil' in the water. Once she has gone the kingfisher flies off downriver. I haven't taken a photo; instead I smile smugly to myself. Why ruin a perfectly good otter sighting by trying to take a photograph of it?

Opposite: **The House female calls to the male inside the nest.** Above: **When judging their dives, kingfishers take diffraction into account.**

For two weeks I watch the same behaviour from the kingfishers – dig, dig, dig. From the gloaming hours before dawn all through the day to dusk, the birds dig, feed and dig some more. I am waiting for them to mate, though – this is the next shot on my list. I have filmed it several times and taken some very bad photographs of it in the past; this year I want the definitive shots. So I wait and I wait. The female will not mate with the male until the nest is almost complete.

When the nest is finally finished it is nearly 1 m (3 ft) long with a chamber at the end. The tunnel leading to the chamber has a slight uphill slope, to help drain it of excreta as the chicks grow. The pair has chosen well – a perfect high vertical muddy bank. Their nest is near the top, underneath an overhang, making it almost impossible for all but the most agile predator to access it. Kingfishers are at their most vulnerable when nesting, so choosing the right location is very important. When conditions aren't quite right and kingfishers are forced to nest wherever they can make a hole, their success rate declines significantly. A high vertical or inclined mud bank with an overhang is the ideal combination and that is exactly what the House pair had. This year, however, the gods weren't on their side.

Left: Kingfisher nest tunnels are sloped slightly to allow excrement to flow out. Towards the end of the nesting period this excreta trail becomes foul. Above: The Manor male with fish ready to feed to female head first.

18 March

The birds appear together, very excited. The male lands in the wood pile at the base of the ash tree and the female on the perch next to the nest. They whistle to each other and the male flutters his wings to a blur. The female then whistles again, single persistent peeps. The male watches her but doesn't seem very interested. She continues to peep and flattens her body across the branch invitingly. He adopts an upright pose before hovering off his perch and going over to her. She flattens herself even more as he hovers above her, then arches her back as he lands on her and takes hold of the feathers on the back of her head. They copulate for nearly a minute, the male flapping all the time to keep his balance. He breaks off very suddenly and speeds off downriver, whistling. The female remains motionless, flattened across the perch for a few seconds, before she rights herself and looks about quietly. She preens for a moment, then speeds off in the opposite direction.

I refer to this pair of kingfishers as the 'House pair', for no greater reason than that their territory includes the river outside my house. Their nest is nearly 1500 m (1 mile) upriver from my house – just below the Manor garden. Not 200 m (200 yds) further upriver is another nest bank, with another pair of kingfishers – the 'Manor pair'. Their territory extends through the Manor garden, upriver and beyond.

The proximity of their nest to the House pair's nest is a highly controversial issue. So as I watch the House female speed off upriver I wonder where she is going and what she is letting herself in for.

The male bird is back 15 minutes later and almost immediately flies into the nest to continue digging. He digs alone for nearly half an hour before the female appears to take over. But she is

not committed and after just two digs she is gone again. The male continues for another hour. I am staggered by his endurance. He eventually stops and sits on his perch outside the nest. He preens for a while, the iridescence of his feathers muted by the earth that coats them. A few skilled minutes and a couple of dummy dives into the river and he is as good as new.

Above: The House male perches on the rocks beneath the nest hole. **Right:** Not all dives are successful!

23 March

I spend a few hours a day with the birds over the next few days and witness three more matings, two by the nest and one at a fishing spot 50 m (50 yds) or so upriver. Most of the matings I have witnessed are around the nest bank, I believe not for any reason other than that the two spend more time there than anywhere else during this period.

Suddenly the river goes quiet. The frequent bouts of frenzied whistling from the House pair are reduced to the occasional peep outside the nest and the odd call as one of the birds zips up the river. The same is true of the Manor pair. This can mean only one thing – the birds are incubating.

Left and above: The male steadies himself by grabbing the female by her head feathers during mating, which can last for up to a minute.

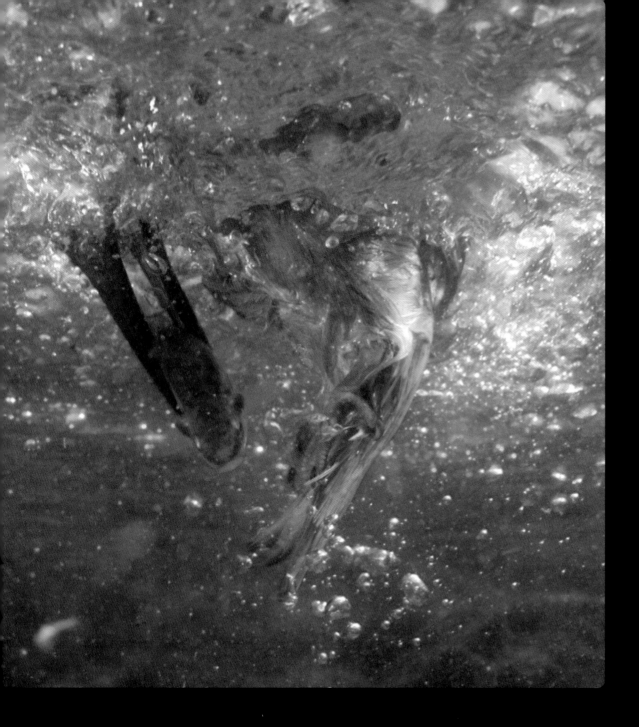

Above: Once the fish has been grabbed it has little chance of survival

A few days after mating the female becomes busy laying her eggs – one small, perfectly white round egg every day for seven days. She doesn't start incubating them until they are all laid, which means that the chicks will all hatch together.

The parents share the task of incubating, sitting for one or two hours at a time in shifts. The female seems to do the majority of it, though, while the male spends more of his time patrolling the territory and fishing. When it is his turn to sit he appears outside the nest and whistles the female out of the hole before flying in himself. She then flies off downriver to fish and preen for half an hour or so before returning, presumably refreshed, to her clutch.

Above: A lucky fish leaps from danger. Note that the blue membrane remains covering the kingfisher's eye.

This is a very quiet time for kingfishers, the month or so from laying to hatching. However, tensions between the House pair and the Manor pair are rising and about to come to a head...

4 April

It's late afternoon. I'm sitting in my hide between the two nests, the House pair's and the Manor pair's. This is a favourite fishing spot for the House pair and they spend a lot of their time here. However it is within sight of the Manor pair's nest and so is a constant bone of contention between the birds. Barely an hour goes by without a loud and aggressive slanging match.

Today seems to be no exception. For almost two hours the male birds from each territory have been pursuing each other at high speed up and down the river. Their whistling is an aggressive rasping – I call it a serrated whistle. This is very definitely a belligerent sound and kingfishers only ever use it when they are chasing off intruders.

The House male lands on his perch near my hide and the Manor male alights on the roots of a sycamore next to the river. Both birds are locked into strange poses, their bodies straightened with arching necks and beaks pointed dagger-like towards the sky. They seem to be in a trance. They lean their necks down towards each other for a few minutes before the House male suddenly launches himself off his perch towards the Manor male, whistling loudly. The Manor male flies back at him and the two try to peck each other in the air before landing next to each other and reverting to the same trance-like poses. Occasionally one gets excited and they burst into whistling before adopting their poses again. They square off against each other with their strange leaning duel for a good 20 minutes, then launch themselves at each other once more. They lock beaks in the air, tumble to the ground briefly to tussle amongst the wild garlic, then roll onto the shingle beach below the sycamore and wrestle one another. Suddenly they break free and chase each other off upriver.

Above: The House male launches himself aggressively at the Manor male.

Above: The two males square up to one another on the border between their territories.

Above left: **When diplomacy fails!**
Left: **The aim is now to overpower your opponent**

Ten minutes later they're back again. They perch on separate branches and shout at each other. Then the Manor male launches himself at the House male and the two birds lock beaks. After a second of flapping the Manor male ends up dangling from the beak of the House male, who remains on his perch. A second later they split and fly up into a blackthorn bush. They whistle aggressively before flying at each other again, locking and falling back into the wild garlic. I watch them hop-fight in the undergrowth for a moment, then separate. Both birds fly and land in the roots of the sycamore, where they retain aggressive postures. The House bird turns and continues his posing with his back to the Manor bird for a minute before the Manor bird flies at him. They tumble down into the river, where they lock beaks amongst the roots of the sycamore. They twist and tug at each other. The House bird seems to have the upper hand and begins to force the Manor bird into the water. There is a brief moment of stillness when both birds, locked together, gather strength and then they continue. The House bird forces the Manor bird backwards into the water and attempts to push him under to drown him, but the Manor bird manages to pull the House bird in too. The two birds are locked by their beaks in the water, they flap their wings and hop against each other, trying to gain the advantage. At one point the House bird seems to be getting the better of it and flaps over the Manor bird, forcing him under. The Manor bird manages to stay afloat and pulls himself out backwards onto a pile of sticks that have collected in the roots. The House bird forces himself up onto the sticks and the two push against each other. They stay locked there for nearly a minute, both exhausted. Then without warning they separate and fly off in different directions, whistling loudly.

Above: The birds hop in the water, each trying to get above the other and force him under.

This level of aggression is rare in kingfishers: most disputes are sorted out by whistling, chasing and posing. However, I have seen several aggressive encounters like this. Perhaps the most memorable was a few years ago when my wife and I were making a film for the BBC about the wildlife in our garden. My wife was at work so I was alone, doing the washing up and looking after our then youngest child Fred, who was still a baby.

For two days I had been watching the growing tension between a pair of female kingfishers as they argued over the nest bank below the weir. Now, looking out the window while washing the dishes, I was sensing that the tension was reaching boiling point. I whisked Fred up, got him a bottle and a nappy and ran next door to ask our neighbour to watch him for an hour while I tried to get some film of the birds arguing. I grabbed my camera and my hide,

clambered into the river below the weir and set up opposite the nest bank. Within seconds of poking the camera lens through the hide window I had both female birds outside the hide. They whistled aggressively at each other and adopted the trance-like poses I described earlier. A male bird, who was busy digging a nest in the disputed bank, appeared from the nest hole and watched for a moment before carrying on with his work.

After a few mock dives and failed attacks the two females flew at each other and locked beaks. They fell into the water and hopped about, watched by a pair of male mallards. They then split and flew onto separate perches. They continued posing and whistling for a few more minutes, then went for each other again. This time they also locked and fell to the water, but one bird had hold of the other's wing, so they didn't hop, they just floated, each trying to grasp the other by the neck to force her head under. It was incredible to watch, but very disturbing as the two birds floated downstream, desperate to kill each other. After nearly a minute they began to tire, both bedraggled and exhausted. They hit a stick in a root system which turned them and gave one the purchase to attempt to escape; then suddenly, with no warning at all, a mink burst out of the undergrowth and grabbed one of them. The other hopped and dived, flapping its wings under the water to help it get away – something I have never seen a kingfisher do before or since. The mink looked straight at me, then swam into the bank with the kingfisher. The other kingfisher landed next to it on a perch and sat there, dripping. The mink climbed a pile of sticks, stashed the kingfisher under it, then immediately came back for the second bird. But by the time it got back to the river the second bird was gone. The mink sniffed about for it, spotted me and vanished.

I had managed to film the entire sequence and my heart was racing about as fast as it possibly could. As I was looking through the viewfinder when the birds were fighting, they were very large in frame, so when the mink burst out it was enormous in my shot. It moved so fast that I had no idea what was happening and went into a sort of cameraman's autopilot. I was shaking so much by the time the mink had stashed the kingfisher that I could barely hold the camera still. It was a very sad moment but an incredible shot.

Twenty minutes after the attack the surviving female was back on the perch outside the nest. The male bird, who had continued digging throughout, flew out of the nest, whistled at her and mated with her. By the time he flew off 30 seconds later she was exhausted and bedraggled. She swayed on the perch for a few moments, then shut her eyes and slept.

The arguments between the House and the Manor pair eased off after their few days of fighting. A boundary had clearly been set. They still crossed each other's paths occasionally, but I didn't see them attacking each other again.

Above left: The Manor male having a good stretch and yawn.

Above: The House male having a break from digging in order to fish.

15 April

The Manor pair is nesting in an artificial nest constructed out of fibreglass by a friend of mine, Jo Charlesworth. Over the winter Jo and I had very carefully measured several disused kingfisher nests to make a mould. He then made several versions out of fibreglass, placed them in wooden boxes and painted them with glue and sand. The result was an almost perfectly lifelike nest chamber. We buried these boxes up and down the river in suitable-looking banks, made entrance holes and left them. The aim was to attract a pair of kingfishers to nest in one of them, and then to get shots of the birds in the nest.

By early spring the Manor pair had taken up residence in one of the boxes and now they are sitting on eggs. It is time to start work. My first priority is to get an infra-red security camera and light into the nest box with video and power cables coming out of it so that I can operate it from a distance. The boxes have been designed to accommodate this rig – the chamber has a small hole in the top for the infra-red light and the side of the nest has a slideable sheet of wood and sheet of glass. All I have to do is get the kit in.

I start by sitting in my hide opposite the nest bank and watching. Jo is in his car 100 m (100 yds) or so from the nest, waiting for my call. After about 15 minutes the female bird leaves the nest and flies off upriver to fish. I get out of the hide and phone Jo. He arrives a minute later and we set to work, lifting up the boards that cover the nest box and the large chamber we constructed for me to work in. Being careful to watch out for the returning birds, I unscrew the lid of the nest box and place the infra-red light inside. I refix the lid and then open up the side of the nest by sliding out the wooden sheet. This reveals, through the glass, the chamber with a perfect little clutch of eggs. Jo quickly drills a lens-sized hole in the wooden panel and I slide it back in next to the glass. I then place the lens into the hole, up against the glass. I power up the monitor, plug the video cable into it and check my shot. A few tweaks and we are done. I drape everything in a thick black cloth and cover the nest box with the boards. We then run the cables 100 m (100 yds) or so away from the nest, plug the monitor back in and wait.

Left: Just before entering the water the kingfisher tucks its wings in and hits the water dart-like.
Above: The kingfisher flaps a couple of times to gather speed before tucking its wings in.

Within a few minutes I hear a kingfisher whistling down the river. Jo and I sit nervously watching the live black and white view of the nest chamber on our monitor. A minute late a kingfisher suddenly appears into shot. It is the female. She shuffles about inspecting her clutch, then sits down on them and shuts her eyes. She doesn't know anything has changed – inside her nest is still pitch black to all but an infra-red camera.

I should add at this point that disturbing/photographing kingfishers at the nest is illegal without a Schedule 1 licence from Natural England. I hold a licence, renewed every year, which permits me to do my work. I don't advise anyone without a lot of experience of working with kingfishers to attempt to photograph them in the nest. It is a very high-risk activity and if done carelessly could result in the parents' abandoning the eggs or hatchlings.

I monitored the nest remotely for the next two weeks until the chicks hatched.

Left: The Manor female searching for fish at dawn.
Above: The Manor male takes a bit of down time during incubation.

Fragile moments

Watching the first few moments of a kingfisher's life fills me with a combination of joy and guilt. It is an incredible privilege, but I keep feeling that I shouldn't be witnessing something so hidden and secret.

1 May

I'm in the Manor garden with my son Fred, now seven. I've just picked him up from school and the two of us have stopped by the Manor on the way home to check the nest camera. As the camera is 100 m (100 yds) remote from the nest itself, we are safe from being spotted by the birds. I plug the monitor into the video cable and power up the camera and infra-red light in the nest. The blue screen flickers and then settles as a black and white image appears – chicks! There is no adult bird in the nest, just seven tiny ugly naked chicks. They lurch about in a pathetic huddle. Fred grins with excitement, although I doubt he realises just what a lucky chap he is to have the chance to witness this.

I hear a whistle downriver and wait. A beak and fish appear in the right-hand side of the shot. The chicks don't seem to react. The female shuffles into shot and stands over her chicks, offering a fish. They appear to have no co-ordination and make no attempt to take it from her. She patiently places it on the tip of the closest chick's beak and waits. The chick eventually finds the right muscles to open its beak. The mother very gently places the fish head first into the open beak and waits as the chick's beak closes on it slightly. She draws back as the chick swallows the fish whole, then shuffles over and sits down on top of her brood; they vanish beneath her feathers. Fred and I watch for a minute or two longer until she shuts her eyes. Then we power everything down and sneak off with great smiles across our faces.

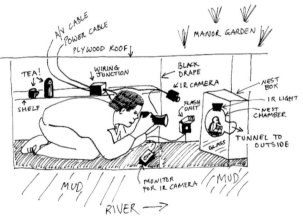

Diagram showing me photographing the nest chamber...

I watch the nest through my remote camera system every day for a week. I am nervous. I don't like working with kingfishers at the nest as the risks of disturbance are so high. As a result I keep putting off the next stage. When I do finally build up the courage the chicks have gained a bit of weight and started to form quill buds.

Beneath my boards is the nest box and a man-sized chamber. This is designed so that I can get into the chamber and photograph the kingfishers in the nest. I spend a day or two sneaking in and out of the nest site rigging it – Jo is always on hand to make sure the adult birds don't show up while I'm at work. After three days of fiddling I get myself in, Jo puts the boards down on top of me and I am plunged into total darkness.

The set-up is simple. I am in a hole about 1.2 m (4 ft) deep and 1.2 m (4 ft) wide. In front of me, about 1.5 m (5 ft) away, is the nest chamber. I have removed the wood from the side of the chamber so that I can shoot through the sheet of glass. Between me and it is a black drape hanging down from the boards above.

My camera is shooting through a hole in the black drape. I have two flash guns next to the chamber shooting through the glass, both wired to the camera. Inside my section I have the camera and various leads powering the infra-red light and an infra-red camera that is firing through my stills camera. I also have a monitor that is displaying the view of the nest through my camera. It sounds more complicated than it is. The main goal of it all is to produce no light visible to the adult kingfishers when they are in the nest.

Above: Female flying into nest with a fish for the chicks. **Right:** Adults' visits to the nest can be as frequent as every 15 minutes.

Above: **The Manor female with fish turned head first, ready to feed to the chicks. Above right: The chicks at seven days old.**

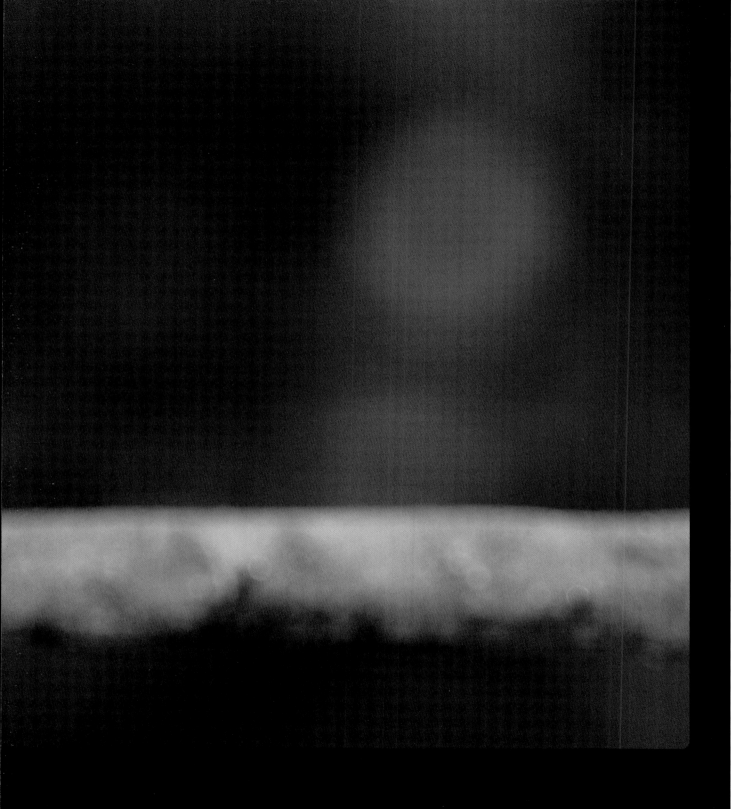

Jo taps the lid goodbye and leaves me, cramped and in the dark. I fire up my monitor and watch the image. I can move and zoom and focus my stills camera and watch the image and the kingfishers won't be able to see a thing.

Five minutes later I hear a whistle, very close to me, outside the nest. I poise myself, ready. I am anxious to see how the birds will react to the flash guns and the sound of the camera shutter. An adult kingfisher appears on my monitor; the picture is not good enough for me to tell whether it is the male or the female. I move my camera on its mount slightly to get framing and attempt to focus the lens. The adult stands above the chicks and offers up a fish. I very nervously depress the shutter button. There is a bright flash and a click. The adult bird doesn't react! I can't believe it. I look at the image on the screen of the digital camera – it's the female and the shot is perfect! I've done it. I turn to my monitor and shoot more pictures. The female feeds the chick and settles down on the brood to keep them warm. I take a few more shots of her and then let her go to sleep.

After half an hour or so the male bird whistles outside the nest before entering. As he nears the chamber he makes a noise that I have never heard a kingfisher make before – a low rasping. The chicks seem to respond to it and wobble about excitedly. The male shuffles forward and offers up a minnow to the chick closest to him. I nervously click my camera again. His reaction is just the same as the female's – non-existent! Instead he waits patiently as the chick tries to open its beak and take the fish. I am astounded by the size of the fish the chicks are eating at this early age. Once the chick has the fish the father shuffles backwards out of the nest and whistles off upriver. The chick lurches back and forth trying to swallow the fish. When it succeeds it goes into a wobbly trance-like state before being sat on by its mother.

I watch the chicks being fed several more times over a three-hour period. The male brings in most of the fish, but every 45 minutes or so the female leaves the nest, returning a while later with fish. After feeding she always sits back on the chicks to warm them up again. They are very vulnerable to chilling at this tender age and it is the mother's job to keep them warm.

Far left: The Manor male fishes relentlessly, minnows being the prey of choice. Left: The female does the bulk of the sitting at this early stage. Above: The female waits patiently for a chick to feel the fish touch its beak. The chicks are blind for their first few days of life

75

Above: Occasionally the male bird would sit in the nest with the female. I never really knew why. Opposite top: The male would sometimes keep the chicks warm, although never for very long. Right: The female would sit on the chicks for an hour or so before going off to fish.

I am ready to leave the nest just before dusk. The female has gone off to fish and I call Jo on his mobile to come and remove me. I shut the kit down, slip out and cover the area with boards. I am aching and stiff from being in such a confined space for over seven hours, but in my mind any amount of discomfort is worth it for the shots I've just captured.

Over the next few days I continue to spend time in the nest, taking photographs of the chicks as they grow. It is particularly interesting to watch the adult birds. Most of the sitting is done by the female; occasionally the male bird will do it, though never for very long. On one occasion both birds sit in the nest chamber together, for no reason that I can see. They remain side by side for ten minutes or more with the chicks beneath them, until the female eventually leaves.

After a week I had to go away filming
and reluctantly left the kingfishers.
A few days later persistent heavy rain
began to sweep in from the Atlantic and
filled the rivers of southwest England.
Eventually the rivers couldn't hold the
water any more and they broke their
banks. All the nests on my river were
flooded out, those of the House pair and
Manor pair included, and a whole nest
cycle was lost. Flooding eventually hit
most of central and southern England
with huge losses of kingfisher nests
all across the country.

28 May

The House pair and the Manor pair are courting again. The House pair has re-excavated an old nest only 1 m (3 ft) from their previous one. The Manor pair has moved upriver almost 800 m (½ mile). I'm working on the House pair for the moment. I have a large metal boat in my garden. It sits on the bank in the paddock and is so heavy that it never moves. A couple of years of rotten leaves sit at the bottom of it and they have turned black, making the water reflect like a mirror. It is the perfect place to get a shot I've had in my head for years.

The kingfishers like the spot where the boat is; the river runs slow and deep there – perfect for minnows. I catch a few and put them into the boat. I'm hoping that the kingfishers will find them and start to use the boat to fish from. Within two days they do.

The metal boat – a perfect studio!

Above: Sometimes even kingfishers get confused. Opposite top: I'm going to have to be quick with my trigger finger! Right: The House female with a very lively fish.

30 May

I get up really early, before the school run, and watch to see who's using the boat. First to turn up is the female. She sits for a while looking for a minnow, but they are hard to spot in the deep dark water. After 20 minutes the male whistles in and lands next to the female. She shuffles about aggressively and tries to shove him off the perch with her beak, but he edges away from her and sits looking into the boat. He very quickly catches a fish and offers it to the female. She eagerly accepts it and swallows it. The two sit together for a moment and then the male flies off, leaving the female to watch the fish in the boat.

The next morning I start trying to get my dream shot, a shot I've had in my head since I was a kid – a kingfisher diving into its own reflection.

The first thing I do is dress the set. I pick some irises from the small stream that trickles into the brook below the weir. I plant these in flowerpots full of stones and place them under the water at the back of the boat. I then dig up some wild garlic and other plants to dress the back wall of the boat. Within an hour it looks like a stream.

I have a small Lego kingfisher that I made when I was a student. It is my stunt kingfisher that I use to plan my shots. It is slightly irritating because it reflects more light than a real kingfisher, but it is a good prop. I attach it to a wire coat-hanger with crocodile clips and position it where I hope the birds will dive. I set up my camera and flash guns and then start to work on my lighting.

I am obsessed with lighting, so this always takes me ages. This time I want a key light, a fill light and a background light. The Lego kingfisher is quite good at showing me how strong each of these lights is when they are working together. I wire the camera into my laptop and take shots by clicking the track pad on the computer. The pictures then appear on the desktop for viewing. This way I know exactly what I'm getting. After an hour or so I'm ready. I plug my cable release into my camera and trail the cable the 10 m (10 yds) back to my hide. Now I just need to sit and wait.

If only real kingfishers were as co-operative as Lego ones!

Left and above: Despite days of trying, the perfect reflection shot eluded me.

It's not long before the male shows up. He peers down into the water and scans for fish. My heart always races at this point. I depress the button on my cable release halfway, ready. He dives. In a split second the camera and flashes fire. He ignores them, too focused on fishing. He has a fish and he kills it by bashing it on the branch. He swallows it, shakes himself and then turns to hunt again. I ready myself, half press the button and... he's in again. I get another shot. He dispatches his fish, eats it and flies off. I jump out of my hide and check my shots – one is good, one is out of frame. I need the bird diving into itself, so I have to hit the button just before the kingfisher hits the water. This is quite hard to judge. I will need to take a lot of shots to get one that works.

I continue all day. The birds don't have chicks, so their fishing rate is reduced to maybe 15–20 fish a day. The male seems to be doing most of the fishing. He's very comfortable with the perch above the boat and spends time there preening and relaxing. Every couple of hours or so the female turns up, fishes and flies off upriver again. This can mean only one thing – she's incubating. It is fortunate that kingfishers can double or triple brood (that is, produce two or three clutches of eggs per year); it means that if they lose chicks to predation or flooding, they should be able to breed again before the season is over. It is great for me, too, because I know that in mid-July the river will be buzzing with kingfishers!

Above: An experienced kingfisher will dispatch a fish with just a few swift blows to the head.
Right: Kingfishers almost always shake themselves off after eating a fish.

After three days of trying, I fail to get the shot I want. I always fail to get the shot I want. I set out with a shot in my head, but unfortunately I work with wild animals whose movements and behaviours are beyond my control, so I almost never get precisely that shot. I find this eternally frustrating, but I have come to live with it. I get plenty of other shots, and in the end I have to give in and accept what I have.

I leave the kingfishers for a few weeks to get on with their nesting whilst I head off to Borneo to work on a film I'm making on orang-utans.

Above: The House male plucks another fish from the boat. **Right:** A failed hunt.

Borneo: kingfisher paradise

I'm not a big fan of rainforests!

I'm in Borneo on a recce. I've been asked to make a film on orang-utans and I've come to travel around and work out the best place to shoot it. So I've got free run of the country! I have a fixer called Cede Prudente, whose job is to help me visit the locations and show me around them. Cede is also a wildlife photographer and strangely enough has a particular interest in kingfishers.

10 June

Wherever I go in the world I am constantly on the hunt for kingfishers and Borneo is a great place to look for them. My recce starts in the north of the country, in the Malaysian province of Sabah.

I'm on my way to Sukau, gateway to the Kinabatangan River. From the town of Sandakan, where I'm based, the journey is two hours bouncing around in the back of Cede's car. The view is mind-blowing. Where lush tropical rainforest once stood, now oil-palm trees stretch as far as the eye can see in every direction. They start the moment we leave Sandakan and end only when we pull into Sukau. It is a depressing sight. Borneo's once great rainforests were some of the most diverse places on earth. Now huge swathes have been logged, burnt and replanted with oil palm for cash crops. Ironically much of the oil from the palm is shipped across the world to be used as bio-fuel!

Despite the complete devastation of the land I spend my time looking out for Collard Kingfishers, which appear on the telephone lines every few hundred metres. I ask Cede to stop occasionally so I can get a shot of one, but every time he does it flies off.

Speed boat — the only way to explore the river systems

Cede rather conveniently owns a lodge on the banks of the Kinabatangan River, so after arriving there and unpacking we jump into his boat, cameras at the ready, and head off. The first life we see is a herd of Bornean elephants swimming across the river. These small elephants, nicknamed 'pygmy elephants', spend a lot of their time in the water and are remarkably docile. We watch them frolicking about for a while and then head off downriver for the more serious business of finding kingfishers. After a few minutes Cede becomes very excited as he's spotted a Stork-billed Kingfisher. We motor over to it, killing the engine as we approach. It is a stunning bird, bright yellow and blue with an enormous red beak. It watches us as we float closer and closer and Cede and I rattle off a few shots before it gets irritated by us and flies off.

Left: **Dawn on the Kinabatangan River.** Above: **The Stork-bills would tolerate us up to a certain distance.**

I think I was more excited by the orang-utans than they were by me!

A few hundred metres below that we reach a bend in the river. Cede gets very excited again.

'Orang-utan!' he shouts.

I look, but can't see it. After a while scanning deep into the bottom branches of a tree with my binoculars I make out the motionless shape of an ape. We sit and watch it for a while and as it relaxes it begins to move and reveals it has a baby. What a treat – a wild orang-utan mother and baby. However, I have one thing on my mind – Blue-eared Kingfishers. These tiny cobalt-coloured jewels haunt the side streams and dark overhangs along the Kinabatangan River and I am very keen to find one.

We head up a small side river. The water is mirror calm and the evening light reflects gold and green from the trees. The constant buzz of insects and the calling of birds are like an orchestra accompanying us slowly down the river. We see Rhinoceros Hornbills, proboscis monkeys, a bearded pig, a cat snake, a couple of monitors and several Stork-billed Kingfishers. Cede shoots everything that moves with his camera and gets some great images of the Stork-bills. I manage a few, but I'm using Cede's camera and struggling with the new functions.

Left: The jewel-like Blue-eared Kingfisher. Above: An immature female Blue-eared.

I hear a whistle, almost identical to my kingfishers back home.

'A Blue-eared,' whispers Cede.

We row towards the sound, scanning the darkness beneath the overhanging branches. A quick flash catches my eye and I hear another whistle. I see it, a tiny black shape in the darkness, obscured by a thousand branches. We drift towards it and when we reach the edge of the branches it spooks and zips off, bursting into blue as it breaks cover and crosses the river. It is gorgeous. Smaller than my birds back home but with a colour on its back even more vivid. It whistles as it crosses the river, then vanishes into the darkness of the trees on the far bank. Cede and I head for it slowly and quietly.

We find it sitting on a thin vine in a small patch of sunlight. We turn the lenses on it, but really struggle to get a clean shot through the tangle of vines and sticks. As the boat drifts downriver slightly I have a clean view and hit the button on the camera; I take six or seven pictures before the view is closed off again by the tangle. We try to manoeuvre into a better position but we're only 5 m (16 ft) away and the Blue-eared doesn't like it; it's off again.

Above: Occasionally the Blue-eareds would let us get really close. **Right:** A brief glimpse and terrible shot of a Black-capped Kingfisher.

We lose it for a while and carry on upriver. I keep
hearing Blue-eareds whistling ahead of us, but when
we get to them they take fright and disappear. As we
near the top of the small river a pair bursts out,
whistling and chasing each other. They land in the
branches of a tree just upriver from us. I watch them
through my binoculars. They whistle fiercely at each
other and then adopt aggressive postures. They pose
to each other for a minute or so before they are off
chasing each other again.

We finally quit in the fading light and head for
home. As we near the confluence with the main river
we spot a Blue-eared sitting low on a branch in the
middle of the channel. We drift towards it. I expect
it to fly off as we come closer, but it doesn't. I watch
stunned as we pass so close that I could reach out and
touch it. It gazes at us, quite relaxed on its perch, not
even flinching. It doesn't look so colourful in the
fading light but I don't care – just to see a Blue-eared
this near is astonishing.

We're off at dawn the next morning. Almost
immediately we spot a kingfisher. It is on a branch
at the base of a vast cliff opposite Cede's lodge.
Cede isn't sure what it is at first, so we motor over
and watch it through binoculars. Cede is thrilled when
he realises it's a Black-capped, a migratory species
that is very rare in the area. We watch it for a while
but it is nervous of us and flies off before we get close.
It is a spectacular bird, with a blue back, black
shoulders and head, white and orange breast and
bright red bill. By this time I'm excited too – we've
seen three species in two boat trips!

Ten minutes later we bump into a Common
Kingfisher. I can't believe it. I've come halfway
around the world and I'm watching a kingfisher
almost identical to the ones I see in my garden. This
is a female and, although the same species, quite dull
in comparison to those found in Europe. Cede
explains that she is probably a rare migrant from
Japan. He gets a few shots. I take a couple, but they're
rubbish. We head up a small side stream and see a
couple of Stork-bills and another Blue-eared.

Above: A Stork-bill showing off his stunning colours.

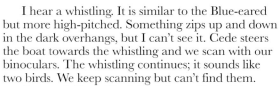

I hear a whistling. It is similar to the Blue-eared but more high-pitched. Something zips up and down in the dark overhangs, but I can't see it. Cede steers the boat towards the whistling and we scan with our binoculars. The whistling continues; it sounds like two birds. We keep scanning but can't find them.

'It sounds like a Black-back,' says Cede. We keep looking and finally we're rewarded, as a bright pink, blue and orange kingfisher flits across the river in front of us. It's tiny! It vanishes into the undergrowth on the other side and we head over for another glimpse, but we've had our luck and don't see it again. Cede tells me it is an Oriental Dwarf Kingfisher, also known as a Black-backed.

The kingfisher I really want to see in Borneo is the Banded. This has to be one of the most glorious of them all, the male having a bright blue back, banded from head to tail with white and black stripes. The female is drabber, with brown bands, but both sexes sport a long, bright red bill and white chest. They live in thick forests and feed on insects, small reptiles and amphibians. Despite hours of searching Cede and I fail to find one – maybe next time.

After leaving Sabah, I go south towards Kalimantan, the Indonesian-owned south of Borneo. I am heading for Camp Leakey, an orang-utan study site in the heart of Tanjung Puting National Park. Like many of the remote parts of Borneo, Camp Leakey is accessible only by boat. The river we travel along is a great place to see Stork-billed Kingfishers and we see lots. However I am not with Cede and the boat driver doesn't share my enthusiasm. So those that I see zip past as the speed boat I am clinging to tears its way up the small waterways towards the camp. I am particularly delighted when a Ruddy Kingfisher flies across the river in front of me, a dazzling display of bright pinky orange. But my sighting is too brief to see more than that.

The Ruddy is my final Bornean kingfisher before I have to leave. I am happy – I've seen seven species in just a few days. When I go back, though, that elusive Banded will be firmly in my sights.

Summer struggles

The river in July is like a dream. She drops to a trickle and the reflections of ash, beech, sycamore and willow that line her turn her surface into a swirl of emerald green. She is the vision of my childhood, of halcyon days. As I stand in the immigration queue at Heathrow Airport I can think of nothing else.

11 July

I'm sipping coffee in the kitchen, fighting jet lag, about to do the school run. A kingfisher whistles past the kitchen window – it has a fish in its beak! The first thing I do when I come back from a trip is find out what my birds are doing. I miss them when I'm away and I am always keen to catch up on the gossip. A fish in the beak means the chicks have hatched. I drop the kids off at school, park the car at the manor and head down to the river with my binoculars and my border collie, Dave. Dave is a lovely chap and often accompanies me on my trips to the river. He is young and fun to be with. My old dog, Bill, died a few years ago. Bill was my greatest companion and was always by my side. I would walk the river with him daily and he would sit in my hide for hours without moving, sleeping with his head on my camera

bag. Sadly, Dave doesn't yet have Bill's patience and he also carries with him a powerful odour!

We walk through the Manor garden to the nest. When we reach it we hunker down in the bushes upriver from the nest and watch. Within a minute the male appears with a fish in his beak. He whistles as he arrives and sits in the sticks below the ash tree. He whistles again as he flies off his perch and vanishes into the hole. He's in there for about 20 seconds and then he's out again, twisting in mid-air as he falls backwards out of the nest hole. In another moment he's off downriver. The chicks are obviously still young. As they get older, feeding time inside the nest will be about seven seconds; this feed took much longer. I'm excited as I head back to the car. I have a whole month of kingfishers to look forward to.

19 July

The sun has been up for half an hour. I'm sitting in my hide. The chicks must be growing well – both male and female have been busy going in and out of the nest since first light. I arrived early and got my kit set up. I'm taking photographs of the adults flying in and out of the nest hole. The set-up is fairly elaborate but the birds take no notice of it. The male looked at the camera and flash guns outside his nest for a moment, but soon decided to ignore them. The female flew up and almost immediately sat on one of my flash heads. Kingfishers don't seem to look at photographic equipment in the same way as we do.

I've got a selection of shots in my head. Today's is a wide-angle view of the kingfisher flying into the nest, with river behind. As usual I am stressing about the lighting. The overhang of vegetation above the nest hole makes the bank very dark, which means I have to balance the light with the background, which is very bright. However I also have to light the bird nicely and light the whole of the nest bank. It is a real headache and I have to keep nipping out between feeds, so that the adults don't see me, to adjust the flash heads. I have five working on this shot: three on the bird and close bank, one on the further bank and one on a broken sycamore branch I've placed in the water at the end of the bank.

The birds are being very co-operative, though, and completely ignoring all the kit and flashes. Each time one of them flies into the nest I take a single shot and each time they fly out I take another. Most of the shots have something wrong with them, most often the bird's wings in the wrong position. I have an image in my head of the position of the bird's wings.

Motion blur...

By 9.30 the sun has lifted enough to bring the shot alive. I am excited when the male bird arrives – this is it, everything perfect. He does his usual routine. Lands in the pile of sticks at the base of the ash tree, whistles, then flies into the nest. I hit the button the moment before he reaches the nest hole, wait seven seconds, poise for the split second when he reverses out, hit the button again and watch him as he washes and preens. He does this for about three minutes and then flies off downriver whistling – same every time. Each time he disappears I jump out of the hide to see what I've got.

The shot looks good on the camera screen. I pop the flash card out, stick a new one in and retreat to my hide to check the shot on my laptop. I put the card in eagerly – I have high hopes for this shot. It loads and….it's not sharp! The shot is but the kingfisher

isn't. I'm gutted. I know what I've done – I've tried something new and it hasn't worked. Kingfishers move very fast and to freeze them in flight you need either a very fast shutter speed or to use flash. I am using flash. However even flash sometimes isn't fast enough. Flash works in two ways – either you set it to automatic and let it do its thing, or you set it to manual and tell it what you want it to do. I always set my flash gun to manual. I then tell it how much light I want it to output – this can be anything between full and 128th power. Usually I set it to 8th or 16th power. This means that it is working at a fraction of its potential; it is, however, putting out a very short burst of light. On full power the burst of light can last up to a 500th of a second. On 8th or 16th power this is reduced to anything from a 5000th to an 11,000th of a second. This is very fast indeed and quite capable of freezing a kingfisher in full-speed action. The drawback of working like this is that the more I reduce the power of my flash guns, the less light I have to work with.

This morning I am trying to balance an almost dark nest bank with a bright river. I've made a mistake, though. I set my flash heads to quarter power, slightly brighter but slightly slower than usual. The result – enough light to light the shot well but not enough to freeze the bird in motion.

The female arrives whilst I'm looking at my failed shot. I gently close the lid of the computer and watch her. She lands on her perch, outside the nest. She looks about for a minute, then thins her feathers and flies up into the nest. I take a shot. She feeds and drops out of the nest. I take another shot. She washes, preens and then she's off downriver. I check the shots – exactly the same problem.

I fix this by reducing the amount of light the flash guns are putting out. I have to make other compromises with the camera to do this, but I have no choice. I continue to take shots all morning until the light lifts off the river, but fail to get the one I want.

I stay at the nest for the next few mornings. Clouds are thwarting all my efforts to get the wide-angle shot – Britain is a very frustrating place to be a photographer. Instead I take close-ups of the kingfishers flying in and out of the nest, with moderate success. Eventually a sunny day is forecast and I try the wide-angle shot again. I get it on the fifth attempt. I check it on the laptop. It's all right, though the morning sun isn't as strong and the lighting on the bird isn't as good as I would like them to be. I continue to try for two more days but the weather closes in and I'm forced to give up – maybe next year.

Left: The House male taking a brief moment to rest after a hectic morning's fishing.

Above: Newly fledged juvenile kingfishers like to sit low and close to the river.

30 July

I'm in my hide in the Manor garden. I say in the garden – I'm actually up to my waist in the river. The Manor pair's chicks have fledged and I'm trying to photograph the adults feeding them. After losing their first broods in the flood, the House pair and the Manor pair both rebred at the same time and their chicks fledged within two days of each other. Once they left the nest, the House pair's chicks moved downriver, into an area between the manor and my house. I never work this stretch, as it is not private. Instead I decide to work with the Manor kingfishers as the land is private and I won't be disturbed.

When kingfisher chicks leave the nest at just over three weeks old they seem to stay loosely together on a specific stretch of the river. These stretches seem always to be the same, certainly with the Manor birds.

Throughout my 20 years of working here, the newly fledged chicks have always used the same stretch, irrespective of which adults are holding the territory at the time and where their nest is. At the top of the Manor garden is a long, deep, dark pool, above it a long, straight, shallow stretch of river. In the straight section is a mass of thick vegetation hanging into the river – brambles, blackthorn and the like. This is where the chicks gather after fledging. At the top of the pool a long, straight sycamore branch hangs low over the water. I have watched adults feeding their chicks on this branch every year for as long as I can remember. All I can conclude from this is that this little stretch of river has the perfect conditions for fledgling kingfishers: dark, thick vegetation with a good supply of fish to practise diving on. The down side is that the water at the top of the pool is deep, but there is no other place to get a shot of the birds on the feeding branch.

Above: Sun shafts at dawn above the Court field.

Right: Juveniles will eat mayflies to supplement their diet, catching them on the wing.

My hide is in the middle of the river at the top of the pool, weighted down with stones from the river bed to keep it from floating away. My camera sits dangerously low to the water within and I sit in my chair soaked to the skin. I buy at least one new pair of waders a year and I'm tough on them. I usually manage to put a hole in them within a few weeks and by that time, inevitably, I've lost the puncture-repair kit. I then keep meaning to buy a new pair, but I'm always too busy and never seem to get round to it. So instead I spend most of the year with wet legs.

Early morning is definitely the best time to photograph kingfisher activity in the summer. The chicks are hungry after a night with no food and the parents are busy fishing for them.

I've been in the hide for half an hour and there has been a chick outside the hide since before I got in. He is very tame – he's just fledged and has not yet learned to be wary of humans. If I wasn't trying to photograph him with his parents I wouldn't need a hide at all. He watched me sneak in and arrange myself and camera, just 3 m (10 ft) away from him, without flinching.

It is a grey, overcast morning. I take a few bad shots of the chick for reference. Kingfisher chicks look much like their parents. They have a few features which set them apart, but the differences are only slight. They are duller in colour, they have very faint grey/blue banding around their chest, they have black feet and, perhaps most noticeably, they have a white tip to their beak. Their most obvious difference, though, is in the sound they make. They don't whistle; instead they make more of a clicking sound, perhaps more like a grey wagtail than a kingfisher.

I hear an adult coming, whistling every three or four seconds as it speeds upriver towards the chicks. The male lands on the perch next to the chick in a hail of excited whistling. The chick immediately clicks at him and shuffles over towards him, begging with an open beak. The male leans in, whistling, and offers the fish. The chick is a bit useless, though, and stabs at the male's beak. The male waits patiently; in a moment the chick manages to take hold of the fish and after a brief tussle grabs it and swallows it. The male immediately flies off, leaving the chick to digest.

Fifteen minutes later the male is back, but this time he lands beneath a blackthorn bush behind me. I peer out through the rear slats of the hide to see him feeding another chick. The chick in front of me flies over to try to take the fish, but he is too late. The male feeds the other chick and flies off again. The two chicks sit together and wait for him to return.

I watch the birds all morning. I take a few pretty rubbish shots of the male feeding the chicks, but nothing of any worth. The perch behind my hide seems to be quite popular, so I decide to focus on it. I move my hide upriver into shallower water, set up a couple of flash guns on the perch and sit draining my waders for the rest of the afternoon.

The perch does indeed turn out to be popular. Soon after I finish setting up, the adult female arrives with two chicks in tow. They land next to her and start begging her for the bullhead she is carrying. She feeds one of them and sits for a moment as it swallows. The other chick continues to hassle her and pecks at her, begging for a fish. She becomes irritated and pecks back. The chick hops away from her, then straight away moves back in to continue begging. The female turns and flies downriver, the chick follows and I watch the two vanish, leaving one contented fat chick on the perch.

Five minutes later the female is back with another fish. This time she has two chicks in tow. They land on the perch next to the hide – suddenly I have four kingfishers in front of me. I excitedly take a couple of snaps. The chicks all beg her for the fish. She feeds one of them while the others squabble. Then she sits for a moment but the chicks pester her again and she pecks at one of them before flying off. Even now, in these early stages of fledging, the mother is becoming irritated with her young; within just a few days she will turn on them and they will be banished from the territory.

Top: The Manor female feeding a chick. Note that both have a protective membrane over their eyes.
Above: It is not long before the female becomes intolerant of the fledglings.

Above: Persistent begging doesn't always pay off. The parents are very good at remembering who's been fed and who hasn't.
Overleaf: One of the Manor juveniles squaring up to an older 'rogue' juvenile.

31 July

I'm in my hide early the next morning. First to arrive on the perch are two fledglings. They sit side by side, bobbing up and down and looking about. One looks a bit more mature than the other – it already has a very slight slither of red on its lower bill, suggesting that it is a female. After a while I hear an adult bird whistling upriver and I ready myself as the male lands on the perch. The two chicks immediately beg for food. The younger-looking one is fed, despite the other's begging. The three birds then sit together. Suddenly and without warning the adult launches himself at the older-looking chick, which tumbles backwards off the perch and speeds away downriver with the male whistling after it in hot pursuit.

I realise what's going on; I've seen this before. The chick must be a rogue from another clutch. This is common at this time of year – older chicks who have been forced out by their parents try to muscle in on another family and be fed by the adults. Often I have seen these rogue juveniles steal fish off the younger resident chicks and attack them aggressively. They are almost always caught, though, and never seem to hang around the territory for more than a day or two. They will fish at favourite spots and vanish the moment they hear an adult calling, sometimes flying over hedges and fields in order to escape.

The chick is soon joined by another. The adult male reappears without a fish. He lands on the perch all fired up and attempts to drive the chicks off by pecking at them. They flinch but hold their ground, shuffling backwards away from him. He settles eventually and relaxes. He catches a fish and feeds one of the chicks. The other one begins to bother him, pecking at him and shuffling closer and closer. He tries to move away, all the time watching the water for another fish. The chick becomes so excited that it hovers over him and attempts to land on him. The male turns and stabs at it aggressively. The chick lands next to him and continues to peck and beg. The male catches a fish and attempts to dispatch it, but the chick is too in his face. Eventually the male flies off and kills the fish on the long sycamore branch before feeding it to another chick further downriver. He then disappears with the pestering chick in tow. This is classic fledgling behaviour. Kingfishers are pretty highly strung and the adults find it very hard to remain patient under such pressure.

Left: Chick begging the Manor male for a fish before he's had time to stun it. Top: A 'rogue' juvenile attacking a Manor youngster. Above: The Manor female getting irritated by her offspring!

A few hours later I'm watching one of the chicks trying to catch fish. It seems totally focused on the minnows below the perch, but despite diving at them relentlessly it can't seem to catch one. After half an hour it is very obviously wet. A few dives later it can barely make it out of the water. It sits on its perch and casually attempts to preen itself, but soon loses interest and locks back onto the fish. It dives again but this time as it comes back up it sticks to the surface of the water. It flaps and struggles as the current begins to carry it downstream to the deep pool below. The chick becomes more frantic with its flapping as the current moves it faster. I scramble out of the hide to grab it, but it manages to flap its way across to a small pebbly beach and sits amongst the undergrowth, shaking. I back off and sneak into my hide. The chick sits shivering for over an hour. Eventually it seems to warm up and finds the strength to preen itself. After ten minutes of preening it looks a lot better and

manages to fly off to a perch downriver. I watch it sit quietly for a while, before one of the adults appears and feeds it. A valuable life lesson learnt!

Kingfisher chicks are incredibly vulnerable at this age and many of them won't live to see their first winter. Drowning is one of the most serious dangers. Like all water birds, kingfishers need to preen regularly. This not only dries out the feathers but distributes oil from the preen gland, giving them a degree of water repellence. Without preening a kingfisher becomes waterlogged and can die. The chicks need to learn this, and bitter experience is often the only way. Adult kingfishers preen all the time, sometimes for more than an hour.

I have found several drowned kingfisher chicks on the river over the years. One was on the beach opposite the nest it had fledged from. I assume it hadn't managed to fly and had hit the water, flapped its way across and died of exposure.

Above left: The Manor male – always on the lookout for fish.
Above and right: Kingfishers preen regularly to keep their feathers in good condition.

1 August

The next morning I'm watching a chick fishing. I'm not sure whether it's the same chick I watched nearly drowning yesterday, but it is taking its fishing very seriously. It dives and catches a tiny minnow. It doesn't bother killing it, it just swallows it whole. It catches another. I'm impressed with its skill at such an early age. The fledglings have just over a week to learn to catch fish before their parents lose patience with them altogether. Some learn early, others hardly learn at all, instead continuing to beg their parents for food until they are kicked out of the territory with few fishing skills – I assume to come to a hungry end. This chick is doing well. Young minnows seem to be a staple on this river. They are slow-swimming and they tend to hang out near the surface. They are, however, small, so it takes a lot more of them to make a meal. The chick spots another fish and dives. It returns to the perch a second later with a fully grown stickleback. Now I'm really impressed. It casually attempts to kill it by knocking its head against the branch, but really just hits its own beak a couple of times, then swallows the fish.

Or rather it tries to swallow, but stops mid-gulp, beak wide open. It tries gulping more and shutting its beak, but it can't seem to do either. The fish is stuck.

Above: Juveniles are soon hunting for themselves. The white tip to the bill, black feet and dark crown around the chest distinguish them from adults.

The Manor male was occasionally camera shy

Sticklebacks have several spikes on their back and sides, and when threatened they stick these spikes out to protect themselves; they are very sharp and I have been spiked by them many times. The chick continues to attempt to swallow, but the fish is stuck fast, spiked into its throat. After ten minutes I begin to worry for the chick – it can't seem to do anything but sit on the perch, beak agape. When an adult kingfisher catches a stickleback it can hit it on the head 20 or 30 times, obsessively whacking it before attempting to swallow it. Now I can see why.

Twenty minutes later the chick is still stuck with the stickleback. It begins to sway and wobble on its perch; now I'm really fearing for it. After half an hour something obviously gives and the chick gulps the fish down. It shakes itself and sits quietly on the perch for an hour before fishing again. For these inexperienced chicks danger never seems to be far away.

I watch the chicks for nine days in total. By the time I finish they are dispersed across the territory. The parents have become almost completely intolerant of them and attack them every time they see them. These attacks aren't as ferocious as those they vent on intruders but they are persistent and do eventually drive the chicks out of the territory.

Above: Sticklebacks can prove lethal to young kingfishers if they are not killed before being eaten.

14 August

For two days kingfishers have been screaming past the house chasing each other. It seems a territorial dispute is taking place. I assume it involves the House pair, as this stretch of river is part of their territory. I'm too busy to take any pictures, so I can't work out who the protagonists are, but I keep my eye on them and wait for the situation to settle. A week later things are quiet again. I notice a kingfisher regularly sitting in the reed bed opposite the house. When I put my binoculars on it I see it is a female. Nothing unusual in that. As she always seems to sit on the same branch I think it would be nice to take some shots of her.

15 August

Next morning I set my camera up on a tripod with a single flash gun pointing at where I hope the female will sit and I wire the cable release back to the kitchen window. I pop the wire through the window, sit on the chair on the other side of the window and wait. It's not long until she arrives. She flinches at first when I take her picture, but soon relaxes. She hangs around on the perch for 20 minutes or so until she catches a fish and flies off upriver.

When I load the pictures up onto the computer later on, I realise that the female is actually a subadult, most probably a first brood from this year. I am amazed. She must be a plucky girl: to oust an established pair from their territory is no mean feat. I am of course slightly sad to lose the House pair – I've spent a lot of time with them over the year – but this young female is obviously a tough cookie and I am interested to see how long she'll stay in residence.

There is a lot of kingfisher movement at this time of the year, when the second-brood juveniles head off to find their own territories; the same is true in early July with the first-brood birds. The young kingfishers either find an uninhabited stretch of river or lake, head for the coast, or stay and fight for a stretch of river. Desirable territories are fiercely protected and the odds are heavily stacked against a youngster wrestling one off an older, more experienced bird. It does happen, though, and on the odd occasion the offspring can fight their parents for the territory and take ownership of it.

The river goes very quiet as the summer draws to an end. The young female holds the territory without contest and I watch her every morning as she fishes the reed bed opposite the house. One of her favourite perches has become the top of one of the enormous spindles that raise the sluice gates halfway across the bridge to our front door. She sits on it almost every morning and looks beautiful amongst the dew-drenched cobwebs backlit by the morning sun. I watch her from the bedroom as I get the kids ready for school, until eventually she spots me and flies off upriver.

The view from the house is stunning in these early days of autumn. Dew from the moist nights drenches the cobwebs which hang sodden in their hundreds across the railings and sluice. The sun rises behind them and they start to shrink, but for a few brief minutes before they're gone they glisten like a million pearls.

I am rewarded in late September by the arrival of a new bitch otter and her cub. My wife and I hear the cub one evening while we're making dinner. We nip out onto the patio with the kids and try to keep them quiet while we watch. A moment later we catch the briefest glimpse of the otters' backs as they nip over the end of the weir race and down the bank to the river below. The cub is not four months old and the mother also looks young.

The otters appear the next night and then most evenings for a month or so, always at around tea time. Often they will fish the weir race in front of the kitchen, oblivious to the powerful floodlight that lights the river, and we will watch them from the patio as they twist and turn in the water beneath us, sometimes just 2 m (6 ft 6in) away.

It's at this quiet time of the year that I am off on another overseas assignment. I'm going search of more exotic kingfishers in a place that puts my little river and weir into a completely different perspective.

Right: A young female takes up residence outside my house.

Above: **Victoria Falls. Not so impressive in the dry season!**

131

Zambezi:
land of giants

It's dawn and I'm in a speed boat carving my way down the Zambezi River, just 1 km (¹/₂ mile) from Victoria Falls. The sunrise is stunning and the Zambezi is like a millpond. We pass wallows of hippos in the water and groups of elephants on the bank. The river is alive with water birds – cormorants, egrets, ibis, darters, herons and kingfishers. They are everywhere, hovering and perching on tall trees, on every bend. This is my first venture out on the river, but I can see that the month ahead is going to be great.

6 October

I'm in Zambia making a film on Victoria Falls for the BBC. As the producer I get to choose what we film and I've chosen lots of kingfishers! My co-producer Jamie McPherson has already filmed Giant Kingfishers courting and I have come out to finish the sequence and shoot some other stuff. My guide and boat driver is Tom Varley. Tommy knows the waters of the Falls better than anyone and can get his boat into places no-one else can. He is also great on birds, so really knows about the kingfishers on the river.

As well as kingfishers I have a long list of other subjects – elephants, the Falls, fishermen, fish eagles and so on – but it is the prospect of filming Giant Kingfishers that excites me most.

This stretch of the Zambezi marks the border between Zambia and Zimbabwe, and the Giant Kingfishers are nesting in a large termite nest at the base of a tree on a small island next to the Zimbabwe mainland. Giant Kingfishers are the largest of the kingfishers and despite their lack of brilliant plumage are still magnificent. Officially I am not allowed into Zimbabwe, as the BBC is banned. However, I figure what they don't know won't hurt them, so I set up a hide. It is a camouflage dome. Camouflage is illegal in Zimbabwe, so hopefully I won't be spotted lurking in it without a visa!

More concerning to me is the amount of elephant poo and hippo prints around my hide. Tommy nonchalantly tells me I have nothing to worry about. He also doesn't seem too bothered by the fact that in order to get to the hide we have to wade through water full of crocodiles! I begin to discover that danger is of no concern to Tommy. It is to me, though, and it occurs to me that working on a small river in southern England has its benefits.

The Giant Kingfishers in the termite mound have been nesting for months. It's September, but they built their nest in June. They mated in July and by now they have three good-sized chicks with quills. Tommy and I find this out by putting a fibre-optic camera into the nest while the parents aren't in. The nest tunnel is an amazing feat of digging. The entrance hole is about the width of a large grapefruit and the tunnel is just over 1 m (3 ft 3 in) long with a substantial chamber at the

end. The termite mound itself is very hard; digging it would have been quite a chore. I have seen a few Giant Kingfishers' nests along the river, but this is by far the best positioned. Many of the nests we've seen are only 30 cm (1 ft) or so above the river and not in a vertical bank, allowing easy access for predators. One had even been chopped in half by an elephant's foot as it climbed down the bank into the river, but the birds were still using it.

Left: A male Giant Kingfisher keeps watch outside his nest. **Above:** Female Giant Kingfisher ready to feed chicks.

7 October

Dawn. The river is alive with birds and hippos. I am not a fan of hippos. They are large and very dangerous; they are also notorious for attacking canoes in this part of the Zambezi and our boat is not much bigger than a canoe. The kingfisher nest in the termite mound is positioned directly opposite the rising sun, so dawn is the time to film it. The birds are very busy and I watch them from my hide. I don't know much at all about Giant Kingfishers, so I am keen to observe and learn.

First thing I notice is how the feeding system works. While one of the adults goes fishing, the other stands sentry outside the nest on a nearby perch. Every half-hour or so there is a changeover. One bird comes back with food for the chicks, feeds them and then stands sentry while the other goes off fishing. This seems to be a sensible plan. A kingfisher as large as this would be quite a challenge for most predators capable of entering their nest tunnel.

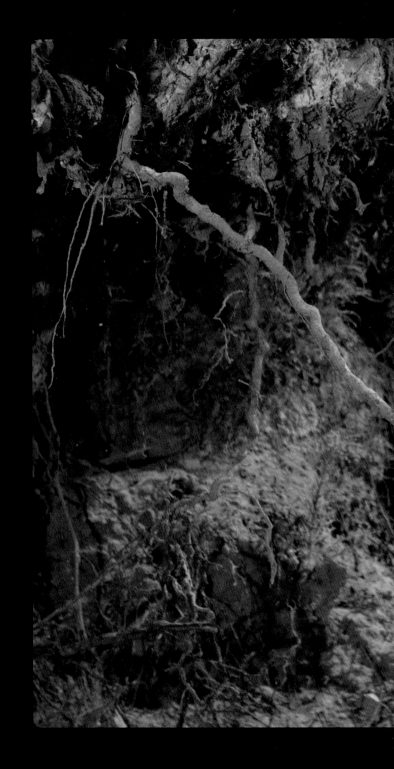

When one of the adults arrives with food for the chicks, it lands on a perch near the nest and calls. The sound is a cackle similar to that of a kookaburra. As the bird prepares to fly into the nest, the cackling becomes more excited and prolonged. I am interested to see the length of time it spends calling outside before entering the nest. Sometimes up to ten minutes. I assume this is so that it can also keep an eye out for predators. When it finally does go inside it is in there for no more than about 15 seconds before flying out and straight into the water to wash. The favourite preening spot is just a metre or so (a few feet) from my hide, so I get some great footage of the birds sprucing themselves up.

The sun is really hot by around eight in the morning and I start to melt in my hide. Stupidly the only fluid I have brought is coffee, which is not the drink to have when you're hot and thirsty. So I sit and swelter as I wait for something to happen. It's not long before I've gathered the standard shots I need for the film – birds flying in and out of the nest, close-ups and mid shots of birds with food, wide shots of birds on the river, shots of preening. Once I have these I am eager to get anything else that is subtly interesting, idiosyncratic, to give the birds character. Unfortunately the birds seem just to stick to their pattern of feed, guard nest, feed, guard nest.

Opp. site: **Female Giant** fly into the nest with fish. Above: **Male Giant having just left the nest.**

Above: I really struggled to get a clean shot of a Half-collared Kingfisher. This one was more accommodating than most.
Opposite: This Brown-headed Kingfisher was pretty relaxed, as it lived in the grounds of a hotel.

Every so often a Half-collared Kingfisher will land in the tree near the Giants, but they ignore it. I watch a Brown-headed Kingfisher hunting in the trees above the nest, but he is ignored too. However, every time a Pied Kingfisher comes into the airspace and lands near the nest area to fish the Giants drive it away, cackling aggressively. The Pied is far more agile than the Giant, though, and isn't bothered by their attempts to shoo it off.

Pieds and Giants are competition to each other. Half-collareds are smaller and eat smaller fish, so the Giants don't see them as much of a threat. The same is true of the Brown-headed Kingfishers, which don't really hunt fish: they are members of the subfamily Daceloninae, forest kingfishers feeding mainly on insects and small reptiles. I have seen them catch both fish and tadpoles, but neither make up a large part of their diet. Pied Kingfishers, however, hunt fish similar to the Giants' prey and although the Pieds are much smaller, they can still take decent-sized fish – fish which the Giants would like for themselves – so when the Pieds come too close the Giants see them off.

I am amazed by the range of food the Giant Kingfishers are bringing to the nest. As well as various fish species, the most impressive being a tiger fish, I also see crabs and crayfish. These are not small and I can't believe that the young kingfishers can swallow them. I watch the sentry bird catching freshwater crabs near the nest. It is great to film. First thing is to remove the legs, which they do by scraping the crab along the branch, then smashing the leg against it, keeping at it until each individual leg has been broken off. Then they turn the crab until it stands upright in their bill, force their beak shut to crush the shell and swallow the crab whole.

Opposite top left: **Pied Kingfishers like to perch high up.** Opposite top right: **We all make mistakes! This bird has caught a stone.** Left: **That's more like it!**
Above: **Classic Pied Kingfisher action at sunset.**

Above and right: **Pied Kingfishers have a much more diverse diet than the ones I watch at home.**

A very happy me on the Zambezi

I leave the Giants after a few days and begin work on a Pied Kingfisher nest just a few hundred metres (yards) upriver. The nest is a perfect vision of a kingfisher's nest – a steep sand bank with a hole slap bang in the middle. I set up my hide and within two days have gathered all the necessary shots. A couple of times I witness something I have never seen or heard of before, which I get very excited about but completely fail to film. The kingfishers fly up high, three or four at a time, all whistling loudly, then one of them feeds another in flight. The two birds swoop up together and exchange fish like a kiss. It is too fast, though; unless I am going to be able to spend a long time trying, it is too hard to film. I assume from the behaviour that what I am witnessing is an adult feeding a chick. Pied kingfishers are more social than the kingfishers back home. They will nest in colonies in some parts of Africa and pairs will even recruit older offspring to help rear a new brood of chicks.

Left: **Female Pied showing single breast band**

10 October

For the first time since I started watching the Pied Kingfishers there are no birds near the nest. This is odd, as up till now there has always been one hanging around, fishing and watching out for danger. I have been filming them using my 16mm Arriflex. It's a great old camera that can shoot at 150 frames per second, which means that when the footage is played back it appears as slow motion – fantastic for hovering kingfishers. For now, though, there are no birds to film.

I look about for them, but nothing. Then I notice something in the nest hole. The nest is a good 25 m (30 yds) away, so it is hard to see what the thing is. I spin the Arriflex round, look through the long lens attached to it and pull the lens into focus – a mongoose! Sitting calmly in the nest entrance is the golden head of a slender mongoose. It turns and slips back down the tunnel out of sight. This can mean only one thing – the chicks are doomed. I whip the Arriflex off the tripod as quickly as I can and swap it for my HD camera. This has an exceptionally powerful lens and allows me to zoom right into the nest. I flip it onto record and wait. A moment later I spot the mongoose stalking along the bushes outside the nest, where it quickly vanishes. My heart sinks. The nest has been predated – bad enough! But I missed the sequence – much worse!

Above series: The mongoose darts into the nest hole. The Pied Kingfishers arrive home a second too late. **Above:** Male Pied showing double breast band.

However, ten minutes later the mongoose is back. And this time there's a Pied Kingfisher on sentry. It goes berserk the moment it spots the mongoose, which ducks and runs as the kingfisher launches itself at it. Out of nowhere two more kingfishers appear and dive-bomb the mongoose. The mongoose runs along the bank, scales down it and vanishes back into the nest hole. The birds respond with angry clicking whistles and hover around the nest entrance.

After ten minutes they give up and settle back in their tree, watching the nest. No sooner have they done so than the mongoose is back. He pokes his head out of the nest tunnel looking for his escape route, but the kingfishers rain down on him and he is forced back in. For five minutes I watch through the viewfinder in amazement as the mongoose makes attempt after attempt to slip away, but each time fails as the kingfishers attack him. I almost feel sorry for him as he scurries backwards into the hole with every angry swoop. Eventually he comes out and snarls at the kingfisher hovering just in front of his face, before finally building up the courage to make a dash for it. He leaps out of the hole and runs into the nearby undergrowth in a split second while the flying daggers pursue him. Then he is gone. I wait for him to return, but he doesn't.

Above: The male fished hard on behalf of his chicks, before the mongoose appeared.

I watch the Pied Kingfishers until nightfall, but none has the courage to go back into the nest. The next morning they are hanging around the nest again, but still no-one will go in. Even more concerning is that the Giant Kingfisher nest nearby has also gone quiet. Where normally I see a bird sitting sentry at all times, now there is nothing, just an empty branch. I can only assume that the mongoose visited in the night.

The level of predation on these nests must be high, especially on the banks connected to the mainland. Above Victoria Falls, where we are, the Zambezi is a mass of islands that many predators cannot reach – these seem to be much safer places to nest.

The kingfishers on the Zambezi are all pretty approachable by boat and I manage to take a lot of photographs of them without sitting for hours in a hide. More tricky are the Woodland Kingfishers. These birds aren't particularly common in the area, but on the odd occasion I see a sudden burst of bright turquoise as they flit between trees in the acacia woodland away from the river. This leads to a frenzied fumble around in the back of the car to get a long lens on, a window down and a good position for a shot. I succeed in the end, but don't capture anything special.

I have to say, Woodland Kingfishers are not the most colourful or exciting kingfishers in the world. They seem to be able to spend an unbelievable amount of time just watching the scrub for lizards and insects to eat and I get neck ache waiting for them to do something. I've watched them a lot in the Masai Mara in Kenya, and there they are almost always found near water; in Ethiopia they were often miles from water, hunting from telephone lines. Perhaps this adaptability to hunt in different environments is the reason they are so widespread and common in Africa.

Left: Woodland Kingfishers are hard to spot around the falls, but common across much of Africa.
Above: Dawn over Livingstone Island, Victoria Falls.

Above and right: Getting a decent shot of a Malachite proved a lot trickier than I had anticipated

Elephants are a constant danger in the water above Victoria Falls...

...if they don't get you, the crocs will!

Not a safe place to rest!

16 October

Towards the end of the shoot I spend a while photographing Malachite Kingfishers, one of my favourites. Malachites are brilliant little jewels: tiny – not much larger than a wren – but brighter and a more vivid blue than the Common Kingfisher, with a gorgeous orange beak. They are difficult to photograph, however, as they are flighty. We shoot from the boat and drift towards them very slowly with the long lenses on. Occasionally we'll find a bird that will accept the boat and let us get close. The results are nice but not too exciting – just portraits.

Jamie and I also spend a few days filming Pied Kingfishers fishing; we have a special new camera which can shoot at 5000 frames per second! This converts a single split-second kingfisher dive into a

two-minute shot. The results are mind-blowing and give us a glimpse into a world that a still camera can't come close to. I really enjoy working with these Pied Kingfishers. They are tolerant and highly active, which means they are always around for us to film and photograph.

It is sad to leave the Zambezi with all its kingfishers. It is a stunning location, with an incredible diversity of animals for such a major tourist attraction. I can, however, live without the crocs, hippos, elephants and Mr Mugabe!

151

Halcyon days

Back home, the weir creates a mist as the air temperature drops. And at dawn, as the leaves of the giant beech tree above the weir begin to turn from green to bronze, the view from the kitchen window becomes incredibly beautiful.

6 November

I'm in the kitchen, my favourite hide. My computer sits precariously on the draining board by the sink. It is wired to the camera which is on a tripod on the patio. There is a new male bird hanging around. He seems to like sitting on a beech branch at the end of the patio and fishing in the slow, deep water of the weir race. This area is very popular with minnows. I cook a roast chicken once a week and, after eating it and boiling the carcass off for stock, I throw the remains into the river for the minnows to eat. They love it and they swarm around the carcass, feeding on it like tiny piranhas. The kingfisher has spotted this and the result is a lot of white droppings on my patio and a kingfisher which hangs around outside the kitchen window.

The view from my kitchen window

Above: A new male has taken up residence outside my house.

Above: Winter comes to the Court field.

This male is new, he's only been around for a few days. The young female who took over the territory in August seems to be tolerating him. There was a lot of whistling and chasing when he first appeared, but things have calmed down and now she just whistles fiercely at him when she passes. Occasionally she stops and poses aggressively, he does the same back and then they part and continue about their day. This male is very pretty, he's obviously been through his end-of-summer moult – something a juvenile born this year probably wouldn't have done yet – so he's got a year or two on him.

Top left: The new, feisty young female in classic aggressive posture. **Left:** The young female dealing with a minnow. **Above:** The new male on one of the floodlights outside the kitchen window.

Having the camera and the computer wired together means that if I need to make any adjustments to the camera, I can do so remotely. The picture appears on the screen a few seconds after I take it, so I can change things without disturbing the bird. It is the perfect system for the shot of the kingfisher in front of autumn leaves that I'm trying to get. The sun rises behind the beech tree and lights it gold in late autumn; however, the sun is moving fast and the light constantly changing, so having the ability to adjust the camera remotely is a godsend. I spend a few days snapping the male kingfisher like this and get a few nice shots.

Opposite and above: The new male spends a lot of time fishing the mill pool outside the house – perfect for photographing from the kitchen!

Right: The new House male sitting amongst sticks that block the sluice gate after a flood.

Winter has truly arrived

December

As I finish writing my kingfisher diary the river is quiet. Its smell has changed and steam rises from the gushing water below the weir. The wagtails flit about every morning on the weir race and the dippers have started to sing on the bridge before dawn. It is one of the most seldom heard but beautiful songs in the bird world. The evenings have drawn in and the otter is bringing her cub past the house at tea time every night to fish in the pool of the race. It's great fun watching them as they twist and turn in the water beneath our floodlight. The young female kingfisher has taken up a roosting position in a squat bush at the end of the footbridge over to my front door. She arrives at dusk every evening and hunkers down on the same tiny branch every night. She is quite oblivious of people coming and going in the dark, just 1 m (3 ft) away from her. I take people out to see her and we shine a torch on her. She doesn't even wake up. I'm hoping this little female will relax with the new male in the territory and form a union with him. It would be great to have a new 'House pair' next year.

Almost time to hang up my waders for a few weeks

Autumn and winter are quiet times for kingfishers. The territorial disputes of late summer are over and won't start again until the spring; the birds have time to relax and regain their strength. I try to do the same. I am a grumpy old man when I'm photographing kingfishers – I become completely obsessed, thinking of nothing else, morning, noon and night. I will go to sleep thinking of my next shot and wake in the middle of the night thinking of another. I spend as many hours as time will possibly allow me in my hide with my camera. When I'm not in the hide I am irritable and cross. So perhaps we all need a break now, a couple of weeks of calm over the winter solstice to relax and recuperate – is that what they call 'the halcyon days'?

Right: The Manor female hard at work!

Photographic Note

My father gave me my first camera, an old Nikkormat EL, when I was 12. My interest in photography grew out of my obsession with kingfishers and armed with my new camera I set out to photograph them. It was seven years before I took a decent shot.

Kingfishers are a real challenge to a photographer; not just because they are small and relatively shy but also because they move quickly. Freezing their movement requires fast shutter speeds, which require lots of light. My river is predominantly wooded, with only a couple of small stretches free from light-blocking trees. So achieving fast shutter speeds has always been a problem.

This was particularly apparent in my early days if I was forced to use flash. Flash is very difficult to master and despite years of trying to get decent shots of kingfishers on film I almost always failed. I can still vividly remember the excited feeling I would have jumping on the bus from the river to the lab to have my pictures processed, and the enormous deflation and frustration when I got my film strips back to see the failed results.

A couple of years at Falmouth Art School sorted a lot of these problems out. I learnt the principles of photography, including how to work with lights and light meters. I learnt to use different formats of cameras and would shoot kingfishers on medium format and even diving kingfishers on 5 x 4 inch plate cameras. However it wasn't until the emergence of high-quality digital cameras in 2003/2004 that I finally had the tool I needed to get the shots I wanted.

Almost all the shots in this book were taken using a Canon EOS 1Ds MK2. When it came out it was by far the best digital camera on the market. It was the camera I had been waiting for, with a picture quality that could rival, if not exceed, film. Now I could set shots up and know with a degree of confidence that my lighting would be satisfactory. This didn't mean it would be right, of course, it just meant the shot would be exposed!

Lighting has been the bane of my life. In 2004 I met Kathy Moran, Senior Natural History Picture Editor at *National Geographic* magazine. Ever since I was a child I have had one goal, to shoot an article on kingfishers for *National Geographic*. Kathy and I went out for dinner and she asked to see some pictures.

'I don't have any,' I confessed. I had been making wildlife films for too many years and had barely picked up a stills camera.

'Well, you can't work for *Geographic* without any,' she said.

So I took myself off to Shetland for a week and shot stills of otters. It was November, so Shetland was cold, wet and dark. I got some nice shots, though, and e-mailed them to Kathy – 'Look what I can do!' She told me immediately to go away and take some decent pictures. So I went away and tried.

Above: Photographing kingfishers can be a hit-and-miss affair. But even this 'miss' produced an interesting effect.

A year later I met Kathy again, this time armed with a portfolio of kingfisher shots. She liked them, but criticised my lighting.

She encouraged me to continue, though, and for two years I sent her my best shots as I got them. I read every book on lighting and I spent time taking pictures of my dog and my kids and everything I could to fix my lighting. Eventually the pictures got to Chris Johns, Editor in Chief at *Geographic*. He liked them and agreed to a development grant, with the proviso that I 'sort out my lighting'. *Geographic* put me in touch with two great photographers, Joel Sartore and Brian Skerry, to discuss lighting and after I had talked to them I tried again.

Chris Johns wanted the lighting on the underwater shots 'dialled down'. Air traps on the kingfisher's feathers when it dives underwater, which really kicks off light, burning it out to white, when you put a flash on it. Brian Skerry suggested exposing for the air bubbles and under-exposing the bird and background. He also suggested fiddling with the flash guns that were lighting the shot, dialling down one, diffusing the other. I tried this and it worked. However it only worked for one shot and despite all my efforts I never managed to get it to work again.

It was this level of perfection demanded by *National Geographic* that really drove me. I wasn't shooting pictures for people who told me how great they were, I was shooting pictures for people who told me how they could be better and this was what I needed. Kathy's persistent criticism of my lighting has done more for my photography than anything else. These days I'm a lot better, but I have a long way to go.

Almost every picture in this book was taken from either my kitchen or my hide. Kingfishers are shy on my river and a hide is essential. I use a selection of lenses. Most of the work from the hide – portraits etc. – is taken with a Canon 500mm lens. This is very expensive but very good. I occasionally use

a 1.4 x converter on it to increase the focal length, but prefer to do without.

A lot of my photographs are taken remotely, using long cable releases between camera and hide. These I make by buying a Canon cable release, snipping it in half and wiring in an extra 10–15 m (35–50 ft) of cable. All the diving shots were done like this. The camera is always very low down on a tripod, often just centimetres from the bird as it dives.

When I photograph kingfishers I use a fish pool. This is can be anything from a washing-up bowl with minnows in it to a gravel pool on the edge of the river, as long as the kingfisher can fish out of it. This means the bird tends to sit in one spot and dive into another. Some people have ethical issues with this, but I don't: I am careful not to harm the fish and I always give them stones to hide amongst and leaves to hide under. I am aware that this method, although good for photography, can influence the birds' behaviour. When watching kingfishers and making notes on them I take this into account.

I have two flash systems. One consists of three Canon flash units – two 580 exs and one 480 ex. These are great little units that work well together and with the camera. They have very useful functions such as high-speed flash, which allows me to photograph a kingfisher diving at a 3000th of a second with a hint of flash lighting, something older cameras never allowed. They also have a second curtain sync setting, which allows me to tell the flash to fire at the end of an exposure rather than at the beginning. This technique is useful if you want to freeze the action but also have some motion blur in your pictures (see the shots on pages 18, 35, 65 and 81). As well as the Canon flash units I have three Vivitar 283s with varipower units attached. These are great old-school flash guns, highly versatile and adjustable. I can use them alongside one Canon flash gun, which allows me four flash guns working together. The only problem with the Vivitars

is that they are old and therefore a little temperamental; they also hate moisture.

The underwater shots are also taken in a pool. For this I put my camera in a Perspex cube, an idea I got from the great kingfisher photographer Paolo Fioratti. The cube is 30 cm x 30 cm x 30 cm (12 in x 12 in x 12 in) with a dome port on one side. It has no top, so I can access the camera and fiddle with it while it is in the cube – I obviously need to make sure the cube doesn't go completely underwater or it will fill up. When using the cube I generally wire the camera straight into the laptop so that I can work remotely. The underwater shots are all flash-lit. As I don't have underwater strobes, I put my flash heads in sandwich bags and carefully sink them underwater. This doesn't always work.

Left: Lighting this shot was almost impossible.
Above: Getting the blur shots to work was very exciting.

Above: The Manor female is a bit scraggy now that she has gone into moult – but still looks pretty good!

Acknowledgements

I have had huge support over the years from a large number of people who have all helped me to follow my obsession with kingfisher photography. Most notable perhaps are the various landowners who have allowed me unhindered access to their land so that I can work in peace and privacy.

As I have worked the same stretch of river for so long now, some of these landowners have become friends and some almost family. So my heartfelt thanks to Hilly and Nick, Bernard and Diane, John and Sue and of course Richard and Stephanie.

Kathy Moran at *National Geographic* magazine has been a huge source of encouragement (and frustration) to me for the last four years. Much of this book is the result of my attempts to persuade her and the magazine that I can achieve the quality of photography they demand. When I started, the pictures quite simply weren't good enough, but Kathy persisted with me and pushed me harder than anyone ever had before. She is a picture editor with a style: a quality usually reserved for the photographer, but one that I admire greatly.

There is a list as long as my arm of other people who have helped me in one way or another. Here's a list as long as my wrist!

Stella Cha, Jo Charlesworth, Jeremy James, Helen Gilks, Jamie McPherson, Nigel Buck, James Chiswell-Jones, Ian Llewellyn, Simon King, Warwick Sloss, Joe Stancampiano, Joel Sartore and Brian Skerry.

For the production of this book I would like to thank everyone at Evans Mitchell Books, particularly Harry Ricketts and Caroline Smith for first going for the idea and allowing me some licence beyond their usual formats to 'show off more'; Caroline Taggart for being by far the easiest and most sensible editor to work with; and Darren Westlake for his skill and passion in laying out the book.

My family all deserve a pile of thanks. Kingfishers are a huge chunk of me and they have had to endure and accept that. My parents have been supporting my obsession since I was seven and still have to put up with it now. My kids Fred, Gus and Arthur have grown up with a dad who is either out taking pictures of kingfishers or up in his office looking at them on the computer.

My wife Philippa needs a special mention. When I am not away filming, I am in my hide. It is hard work getting three kids up, fed and taken to school while your husband sips coffee in his hide. She accepts this and she accommodates it. Sometimes she'll literally have to drag me from my hide by the ear, show me my children and force me to be a good father. These instances are rare, though, and more often than not I return home after a dawn shift to a strong cup of coffee, a bacon sandwich and a smile.

A well-earned cup of tea in my hide

I will never get bored with watching kingfishers. Time has proved that to me: when there is one sitting outside the kitchen window the whole world can go to hell while I stand motionless and watch it, hoping it won't spot me and fly off. I keep saying to myself that I've done kingfishers now, I should move on to something else, but I know that come the spring I'll hear that whistling as the pair start bonding again and I won't be able to help myself. I will probably be photographing kingfishers for the rest of my life – always chasing that 'perfect' shot. I haven't got it yet and I probably never will. But I can't think of a nicer way to spend my life than chasing that particular kind of gold at the end of the rainbow.